THE NORTH & WEST ROUTE

VOLUME 3B

ABERGAVENNY
MONMOUTH ROAD
TO
MAINDEE JUNCTION

by
JOHN HODGE

WILD SWAN PUBLICATIONS

ISBN 978 1 905184 92 7

DEDICATION

This volume is dedicated to my late brother Albert. It was he who introduced me to the basics of photographic development and printing, which I have now been doing for some 60 years. From the early box camera and primitive enlarger that I used back in 1950, the change to the modern digital cameras and computer scanning which I now use is astounding.

Designed by Paul Karau
Printed by Amadeus Press, Cleckheaton

Published by
WILD SWAN PUBLICATIONS LTD.
1-3 Hagbourne Road, Didcot, Oxon, OX11 8DP

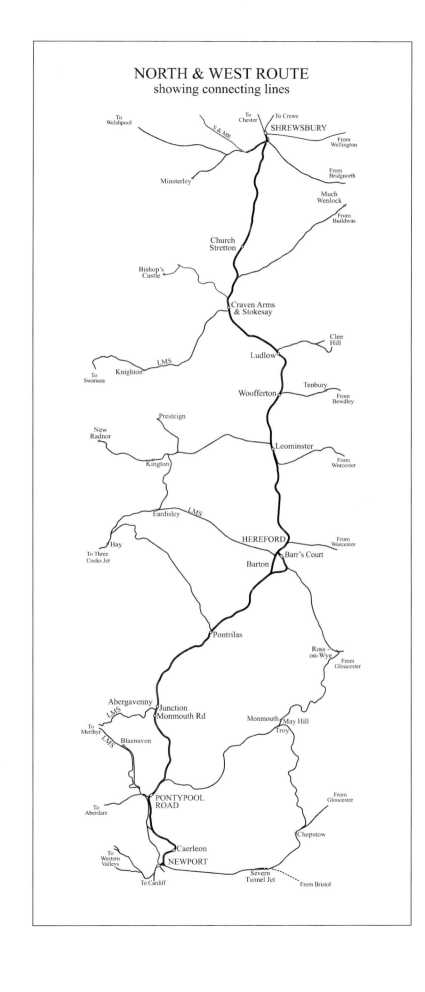

Abergavenny (GWR) station in 1922, looking south towards Pontypool Road. Taken from the north end of the Down platform, this view shows the substantial station building on the Up platform, and the modest waiting shelter on the Down, with the single-bay line to its rear face. The footbridge carried public and passenger traffic over the lines, connecting the station forecourt, both platforms and a footpath along the eastern side of the line. The North signal box can just be seen on the Up platform, beyond the footbridge, with the goods shed forming the backdrop.   LENS OF SUTTON

ACKNOWLEDGEMENTS

I am as ever very grateful to John Copsey for his contribution to the historical text, traffic details and captions in this volume. Also to members of the Abergavenny Railway Society – Nigel Lewis (Chairman), Robin Smith, Ralph Charles, Stan Brown and David Bowen for their help with photographs of the Abergavenny area, and to the latter two for provision of the John Beardsmore collection of negatives for me to print.

The appropriate volumes of Tony Cooke's invaluable *GWR Layouts* have also been widely consulted, and Tony has also kindly provided additional material for specific aspects.

BIBLIOGRAPHY

The detailed story of the Taff Vale Extension and Vale of Neath Lines is well recounted in the *Vale of Neath Line* by Gwyn Briwnant Jones and Denis Dunstone (Gomer Press 1996), and has been studied for aspects affecting this volume. My own copiously illustrated volume(s) on the Vale of Neath will appear when we produce our Valleys series.

INTRODUCTION

Volume Three of this North & West series deals with the section from Hereford to Newport (Maindee Junction). Volume 3A dealt with Hereford to Abergavenny Junction, and this Volume 3B continues from Abergavenny (Monmouth Road) to the Maindee Junctions which linked the North & West line to the South Wales Main Line, the East Junction taking trains toward the Severn Tunnel and the West of England, and the West into Newport High Street and onwards to Cardiff and West Wales.

The branch lines that deviated from or impinged upon the North and West line are described, viz. the Little Mill to Monmouth line; the Taff Vale Extension/Vale of Neath line; the Pontypool, Caerleon and Newport line, which became the main line south of Pontypool; and the Eastern Valley service, which used the North & West between Newport and Llantarnam Junction on its way to Pontypool (Crane Street) and Blaenavon. All these lines combined to add local interest to the main line, where gleaming 'Castles', 'Britannias' and 'Kings' could be followed by doughty panniers bustling along with auto trains or other types of stopping services, with the interminable flow of coal and general freights that South Wales was all about.

BRANCH LINES AND OTHER ROUTES
Little Mill Jct. to Monmouth

The Coleford, Monmouth, Usk & Pontypool Railway opened their branch between Little Mill Jct. (1¾ miles north of Pontypool Road station) and Usk on 2nd June 1856, and this was extended to Monmouth (Troy) in October 1857, with three or four trains a day to and from Pontypool Road, and modest traffic levels.

In 1876, services were still quite modest, with four passenger or mixed trains and one return goods service between Pontypool Road and Monmouth, and a couple of conditional goods services between Pontypool Road and Usk.

By the new century, the branch services had expanded as the system was enlarged, and trains now operated between Pontypool Road and Usk, Monmouth and Ross-on-Wye as well as to Chepstow and Severn Tunnel Junction. The stock was also used for trips over the Coleford branch. Engines operating the line were the '517' class 0-4-2T, 0-6-0 tanks of the '655', '1016' and '1076' classes, and MR&CC designs. The service settled at six trains each way between Pontypool Road and either Monmouth or Ross, with one late-evening train only to Usk.

In the early 1920s, there were seven Down and eight Up Monmouth branch services, operating to and from Usk, Monmouth or Ross. At that time, steam railmotors ran a couple of these services, with a single car based at Pontypool Road. From 1928, auto trains were introduced, the steam railmotors (Nos. 30, 69 and 79 being based at Pontypool Road in 1929) surviving until 1932, after which auto cars provided all regular weekday services.

Diesel railcars arrived at Pontypool Road during 1936, and were soon running on a return Newport, Pontypool Road, Monmouth, Chepstow and Severn Tunnel Jct. duty alongside the auto trains.

In the late 1930s, an ordnance factory opened at Glascoed, just west of Usk, served initially by dedicated passenger and auto workmen's trains from the Newport, Blaenavon and Pontypool areas, running to the new Wern Hir Halt. It was also served by some of

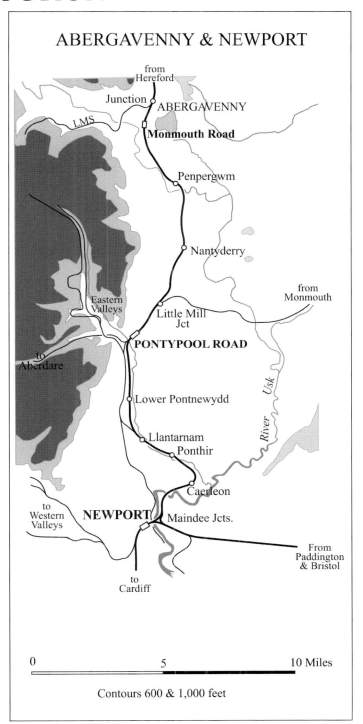

the regular auto and diesel railcar trips between Pontypool Road, Monmouth and Ross. From 1940, the workmen's trains began running into the Glascoed Ordnance Factory branch station, operating for each of the three shifts, hauled by '51XX', '56XX' and '57XX' engines. On the autos, '64XX' and '48XX' were in use.

The Pontypool Road & Monmouth branch services survived only until May 1955, finally worked by a diesel railcar on four return trips per day. The Glascoed services, however, continued with four trains per day for a one-shift operation, running from and to Brynmawr, Ystrad Mynach, Newport/Blaenavon and Rhymney. The trains were worked by incoming Valley and Newport engines, and the return trains, some of 8-coach lengths, were double headed because of the Valley gradients. These services continued until August 1961. Freight services continued to run to Usk until 1965.

Taff Vale Extension/Vale of Neath Pontypool Road to Aberdare/Neath/Swansea (see also NA&HR and Further Development sections in Part One)

The line from Pontypool to Crumlin opened for traffic on 20th August 1855, initially with three passenger trains in each direction, seven days a week. The extension to Tredegar Jct. in June 1857 saw an increase to four, with a late-night Saturdays-only service. The line was opened to Quakers Yard in January 1858, and included a connection there with the Taff Vale to Merthyr, with a couple of trains appearing to run through.

Goods traffic developed quickly, and by April 1858 coal from the Merthyr area was passing over the TVE to Pontypool Road, thence to Hereford and Oxford, whilst other regular traffics were now being conveyed over the NA&H. In some respects, this line was operated as a continuation of the Hereford & Pontypool Road main line.

In May 1860, an excursion train was run from Ebbw Vale to Pontypool via the new Llanhilleth incline, which linked the Western Valley line south of Aberbeeg with the TVE line at Crumlin. NA&H locomotives available at this time included 2-4-0 and 0-4-2 tender passenger engines, and 0-6-0s on goods. By this time, passenger services over the Taff Vale Extension were being operated separately (though in close connection with) the main Hereford & Pontypool Road (and Newport) line. However, goods trains were – and would continue to be – closely associated with main-line traffic, with through running still much the order of the day.

Under the West Midland, there were three passenger trains each way between Pontypool Road and Merthyr, all connecting with Worcester & Newport (Mill St.) services. The calls at Pontypool Road suggest that the main trains ran to and from Newport, but it is quite likely that through vehicles to and from Merthyr were still involved.

There were mineral trains running each way between Dudley and Merthyr, and between Hereford and Quakers Yard. Coal was conveyed eastwards along the line for Birkenhead and Paddington specifically, and on the other trains for destinations in the Midlands. In all, there were seven booked westbound goods, mineral and empties, and nine eastbound mineral or mineral and goods services passing Pontypool Road for and from the branch.

To the north-west of Quakers Yard, on the far side of the high ground separating the Taff and Cynon Valleys, was Aberdare, the terminus of the Vale of Neath broad gauge line from Neath, with its short mineral line extension eastwards to Middle Duffryn colliery. It was the Aberdare district that was the final destination of the NA&H line, and with the completion of the Cefn Glas single-line tunnel, carrying the final part of the NA&H branch between Quakers Yard and Middle Duffryn, the extension was opened on 18th April 1864. The VoN line from Middle Duffryn to Neath and Swansea (Wind St.) was converted from broad to mixed gauge at the same time, permitting the through running of 'narrow' gauge goods traffic

Pontypool Road station, seen around the turn of the century from the south end of the Down platform, looking north towards Abergavenny. The main building is to the right, served by a roadway from the main Newport to Pontypool road that passed over the railway by the roadbridge beyond the station. North box can be seen through the arch. The bay to the right served the Panteg (Eastern Valley) and Newport (PC&N) routes, with a local train in evidence, whilst the bay line on the outer face of the Up island platform opposite probably housed the Taff Vale Extension trains.

The new station was built to the north of the roadbridge, from which this view was taken soon after the building work. The three main lines at the south end can be seen in the foreground against the platform faces, namely (from the left) the Up Main Platform, VoN Bay and the Down Main Platform, with the Up and Down through lines outside them. Goods avoiding lines to the left have yet to be completed. The tall signal in the foreground with a cross on the arm was left over from the old arrangement, and can just be seen over the roadbridge in the early station photograph, whilst the old North box can be seen on the bottom left-hand corner.

between Hereford and Neath, and passenger trains from 5th October 1864.

With the development of all the various links with the north to south valley lines, the Taff Vale Extension assumed its planned proportions, resulting in the considerable expansion of Pontypool Road as a marshalling point for traffic off the TVE line for all destinations. The VoN company merged with the Great Western in 1865, and Paddington extended its influence into more parts of South Wales.

In 1866, with the through line in operation, three passenger trains continued to run each way between Pontypool Road and Swansea (Wind St.). A periodic weekend excursion between Pontypool Road and Neath Jct. (for New Milford) also appeared, though this required a change of train onto the broad gauge at the latter point for travel to the west.

However, it was the goods services that underwent the greatest change, with around 23 westbound and 18 eastbound booked trains running to, from or through Pontypool Road. Coal trains largely originated at Aberdare, Mountain Ash, Rhymney Jct., Quakers Yard and Llanhilleth, being destined for Birkenhead, Hereford and the Midlands, Newport and London, with balancing empties. There were also goods services between Birmingham and Swansea, and Birkenhead and Merthyr.

The change of gauge from broad to 'narrow' on the South Wales main line in 1872 allowed the three trains each way between Pontypool Road and Swansea to run to and from the GWR High Street station, instead of Wind Street, this being rather more convenient for the west. In order to do so, the trains now used Neath (GWR) station, gaining access to the main line at that point.

At this time, large amounts of coal and iron traffic, goods and empties passed either via Pontypool Road Yard or direct to and from the TVE and VoN, including some ten coal trains daily to Swindon, Basingstoke and London, with additional conditional services. These conveyed domestic and industrial coal, and loco coal to the many GWR and Southern Railway companies' depots in those areas, with balancing empties westbound. Most of these services ran from and to Aberdare, calling at Pontypool Road only when required.

Considerable volumes of coal were also conveyed to Birkenhead Docks for shipment and bunkers, usually making brief calls at Pontypool Road yard. In addition, there were some 25 daily services at Pontypool Road yard over the TVE and VoN, with trains to and from Crumlin Jct. and the Western Valley, Maesycwmmer, Rhymney Jct., Llancaiach, Quakers Yard, Mountain Ash, Aberdare and Hirwaun.

A change was made in the early 1880s with the transfer of the London, Swindon and Aberdare coal trains from the Pontypool and TVE line onto the Gaer Jct., Western Valleys, Nine Mile Point (L&NW) and Sirhowy Jct. route. There was still considerable traffic over the eastern section of the TVE, but it was now largely concerned with destinations to the North, and for those collieries around that part of the line. Newport (East Usk) yard now handled some of the through traffic from and to the east.

Engines on the passenger trains in the early 1890s were largely tank, with '1016' and '1076' classes dominant. By the end of that decade, 'Standard Goods', '2301' and 'Beyer' 0-6-0s were also recorded, along with '481' class 2-4-0s.

In 1914, there were five passenger services each way between Pontypool Road and Swansea via Aberdare, with trains dedicated to

Pontypool Road yard, looking north, probably from the Union Road 'viaduct' bridge in the early 1920s. The south face of the engine shed, with its eight entrances, features to the right, and contained a good selection of vintage goods and shunting locomotives. In the left foreground are the Middle Sidings, with the Birkenhead and South (nearest the shed) Sidings beyond, a pair of goods running lines separating them. Middle Junction box is on the extreme left in the distance, with the loop lines to the Vale of Neath curving around to the left beyond it. The industrial sites to the north of the VoN main lines form the backdrop in this view.

Coedygric Junction, looking north, with Coedygric Junction box to the right of centre, framed by signals and telegraph poles. The Eastern Valleys line is seen running to the left at bottom left, with the old, original connection to Pontypool Road curving gently off to the right, and the Old Yard Sidings sandwiched between, on the left. Immediately beyond the Old Yard a cutting can be seen, carrying the Goods lines from Panteg Junction (on the PC&N) into the yards, with the overbridge to its right. The old buildings to the right may have been part of the old Monmouth R&C engine shed, with a '31XX' shunting in front. The Union Road viaduct forms the backdrop in the middle distance; the building just seen above the Old Yard, and on the near side of the viaduct, was the southern end of the Tranship shed.

the route, or running through from the Monmouth line. In addition, five steam railmotor trips operated to Hengoed, Nelson & Llancaiach, Quakers Yard and Aberdare.

There were 16 regular goods and mineral trains over the line, including a through Bordesley and a Pontypool Road (starter) vacuum service to Swansea, but many more conditional movements. A few ran the length of the line, though most were destined for shorter trips to Ebbw Vale, Rhymney, Aberbargoed, Quakers Yard, Merthyr, Aberdare, etc.

Much use was still made of the '1076' class 0-6-0T for working both passenger and coal services over the route, engines often being paired to work the heavier coal services. Various other types of saddle and pannier tanks were used with many varieties of 0-6-0 tender engines.

From the early years of the new century, the new 'Aberdare' class 2-6-0s and also the 'Kruger' 2-6-0s and 4-6-0s were involved in the working to and from the main line. Some of the coal services on the eastern part of the TVE were hauled by the new '42XX' class 2-8-0Ts, designed by the GWR specifically for colliery to yard working; these, however, were not ordinarily allowed over the Crumlin viaduct. '36XX' and '39XX' tanks were also involved in the passenger working.

During the 1914–18 War, much of the steam coal destined for the British fleet at Scapa Flow passed from the Aberdare area collieries via the TVE line, and given the importance of Aberdare depot as the primary source of freight power over the line, it seems probable that the originating through trains were hauled by Aberdare-based '28XX' engines and crews as far as Chester/Warrington, in addition to those trains starting from Pontypool Road.

From the Grouping in 1922, there were nine passenger services in each direction at Pontypool Road, bound for or from Aberdare, Neath or Swansea. In addition, local auto, passenger or steam railmotor trips ran to Nelson and Oakdale Colliery with miners' trains, and also to Crumlin Valley Colliery Platform serving Hafodyrynys Colliery. Five railmotor services also ran between Pontypool Road and Clarence Street to additionally serve the town, and perhaps to allow connections with Eastern Valley services at Crane St. (to Abersychan, Blaenavon and Brynmawr), where 13 trains ran each way per day. Six connecting services also ran between Pontypool Road and Panteg to feed into some of the Eastern Valley trains, and serve the Panteg Works, the service being worked by both railmotors and conventional trains for the one-mile journey.

From April 1928, the line over Crumlin Viaduct was singled for engineering reasons, producing intense delays to trains in both directions as they waited line clear to cross.

The 1930s saw through vacuum goods services from Birkenhead and Bordesley to Swansea run over the line. However, the majority of the traffic was from and to Aberdare, though with many shorter trips from Pontypool Road yards to destinations along the line, and via the connections with the various Valleys. Several services each day ran to and from Aberbeeg, Ebbw Vale and Abertillery in the Western Valley, Oakdale Colliery via Penar Jct., Rhymney via Hengoed, and Merthyr via Quakers Yard, but there were also trains to and from Porth and Ferndale with coal traffic, empties and pitwood which took a circuitous route via Hengoed, Ystrad Mynach, Aber Jct., and Pontypridd (via the PC&N). More locally, coal and empties ran between Pontypool Road and Cefn Crib.

Passenger services over the line now had '45XX' class 2-6-2Ts, along with '57XX', '2721' and '1076' class 0-6-0 tanks. Freights were hauled by classes including '30XX', '42XX', '43XX', '2721', '1076', '56XX' and '57XX'.

Freight services over the line – now referred to generally as the Vale of Neath throughout – continued in this vein throughout the 1950s, though at a reducing level, due to colliery closures, largely through exhaustion. Most general freight traffic now ran via the main line through Newport and Cardiff, and WR management began to view the future of secondary routes such as the Vale of Neath with interest when it came to reducing costs. Civil engineering costs were high on this route, with several areas where long-standing subsidence problems existed due to underground colliery workings, one example being in the Middle Duffryn/Lletty Shenkin area, near Mountain Ash.

The passenger service around 1950 was quite buoyant, with eight passenger trips to Aberdare, Neath or Swansea, and two auto trips to Nelson and Neath, with the balancing eastbound trains. In addition, there were a small number of workmen's trains, both local and the through workings for Glascoed. In the early 1960s, however, the service had become a ragged affair, with little to attract traffic, and it never benefited from the introduction of DMUs. With little apparent interest from management in that developing age of road transport, despite the number of important towns served along the line and a possibly untapped potential, it was no surprise when the route appeared on the planned closure list under the Beeching proposals. In 1964, the line was closed as a through route, passenger services being discontinued and the freight (largely coal) trains diverted to run via the Valley links through Radyr and Rogerstone yards, or on the main line.

During the 1950s and 60s, motive power on the passenger services was provided by Pontypool Road ('43XX', '41XX', '56XX', '57XX'), Aberdare ('56XX') and Neath ('41XX', '81XX'). Freight services were mostly covered by Aberdare using '28XX', '42XX', '56XX' and '57XX', with Pontypool Road using '42XX' and '72XX' (on the Ebbw Vale services, as they were not permitted over the viaduct – although they had been for a brief period in and following the Second World War), '56XX' and '57XX'. Stanier '8Fs' were seen daily on the through Hereford to Llandilo Jct. freights. Glascoed workmen trains using the line were normally hauled by '41XX' and '56XX' engines, assisted on return by '57XXs'. Excursions to Barry Island and Porthcawl along the line were normally hauled by '41XX', '56XX' and '57XX' (double-headed to Porthcawl).

Eastern Valleys

The Eastern Valleys line was intimately connected with operations over the NA&H from the earliest years. At the beginning, NA&H services utilised the connection at Coedygric Jct. to gain access to the Monmouthshire Railway & Canal company's line for the final seven miles into Newport Mill St. station (as did the L&NW by its 1863 agreement with them). NA&H services over the MR&CC line into Mill St. commenced on 2nd January 1854 with four trains from Shrewsbury and one from Hereford, with a similar arrangement northbound. By West Midland days, this had risen to six passenger movements each way.

In 1866, the MR&CC line supported eight GWR passenger trains each way between Pontypool Road (and beyond) and Mill Street, and four goods services in each direction at Dock St., as well as a couple of coal or empties from and to Aberdare and Mountain Ash. The L&NW operated one passenger train each way at Mill Street, and three goods in each direction at Dock Street. It also saw four MR&CC passenger services each way for Blaenavon, plus goods and mineral trains.

The GWR workings into Mill Street and Dock Street continued until the opening of the Pontypool, Caerleon & Newport line from Pontypool Road to Maindee in 1874; this had connections from both the West (Neath) and East (Hereford) Junctions at Pontypool. From that time, GWR passenger services were diverted via the PC&N into an enlarged High Street station, although the

MR&CC line into Newport still hosted up to eight GWR goods trains (Pontypool Road or Aberdare), three L&NW passenger and two L&NW goods services each way.

From 1875, the MR&CC was worked by the Great Western, and in 1880 amalgamated with it. Just before the amalgamation, the GWR opened a new branch between Cwmbran (MR&CC) and Llantarnam (PC&N), in April 1878, enabling trains from Blaenavon and Pontypool (Crane Street) to also use the new route into High Street, although the five daily trains continued to use Mill Street until the end of July 1880. On 1st August 1880, Mill Street was closed to passenger traffic, and the line between there and Cwmbran Jct. became a goods-only line, much used for coal traffic into Newport Docks from the Eastern Valley and Brynmawr in later years.

By 1883, eight passenger trains ran each way between Blaenavon, Pontypool (Crane St.), etc., and High Street, utilising the Cwmbran branch and the PC&N for the final $6\frac{1}{2}$ miles into Newport; these were still being worked by MR&CC 0-6-0 tanks. A couple of local goods services to and from East Usk also used the link.

Eastern Valley traffic over the southern end of the N&W grew, and by 1914 there were around 15 passenger services in each direction, to and from Pontypool, Brynmawr or Blaenavon. In addition, around five through goods trains to and from Severn Tunnel Jct., Newport and Cardiff for the Valleys also utilised the line daily. One or two passenger trains between Newport and Pontypool Road (etc.) were also routed daily through Llantarnam Jct., Panteg (MR&CC) and Coedygric Jct. en route.

By this time, there were around seven steam railmotor trips between Pontypool Road and Panteg each way, connecting with Eastern Valleys services.

'1076' class engines were favoured on the passenger services to Blaenavon, although '44XX' 2-6-2Ts were also utilised. The proto-type small 2-6-2T No. 115 (later 4400) was based at Blaenavon from new in 1904 (along with No. 3106 (later 4406) between 1906 and 1908) to work the Eastern Valley trains, until 1912, at which time they were both at Tondu.

In 1933, auto trains were introduced on virtually all Eastern Valley trains, and covered the Newport, Brynmawr and Blaenavon services as well as the intermediate and connecting services out of Panteg, Pontypool (Crane St) and Pontypool Road. These were hauled initially by auto-fitted '2021' class 0-6-0PTs, then by '1076', and from the mid-1930s by '64XX' class engines. The only conventional passenger trains over the former MR&CC were a handful of daily Cardiff, Merthyr or Newport and Pontypool Road (etc.) services, plus a few weekend trains. The overall level of these branch trains over the south end of the N&W was much the same as in 1914.

The auto trains on Eastern Valley services continued throughout the war and into the Nationalised era, again with around 15 trains each way daily, although the Brynmawr trains had been withdrawn in 1941 and the Blaenavon increased. Once more, there were the through trains between Newport and Pontypool Road using part of the MR&CC route, amounting to around four daily in each direction. '64XXs' again were used on the auto services, but with '51XXs', '56XXs' and '57XXs' when run as conventional passenger trains. '57XXs' and '42XXs' operated the freights. Coal services from the Eastern Valley pits (especially at Blaenavon) were worked by Pill depot.

The Eastern Valleys passenger services were withdrawn on 1st April 1962, still operating with the full Blaenavon service to the last.

Coal services continued to use the Eastern Valley route until the closure of Hafodyrynys Coal Preparation Plant and Blaenavon, the latter in 1980, following which the site of Blaenavon Big Pit has become a heritage site, and a small preserved railway created.

The south face of the engine shed once more takes the centre ground in this late-1930s view of the eastern side of Pontypool Road yards, looking north. The main line (PC&N) is seen to the right, with East Junction box in the middle distance and the old Down side yard to its right, housing some coaching stock. Pontypool Road station was around the right-hand bend in the distance. To the right of the two engine shed blocks can be seen the eastern part of the roundhouse, with its central, single internal turntable. The Coedygric (left) and New Sidings are seen in the foreground. On the upper left-hand side, West Junction box, highlighted by sunshine, marks the point of diversion of the goods loop (to Middle Junction box and the yards) from the Vale of Neath main lines.

STEPHENSON LOCOMOTIVE SOCIETY

About a mile to the north of Monmouth Road station was the former L&NW/LMS station of Abergavenny Junction, which served the Merthyr, Tredegar & Abergavenny branch owned by those concerns (see Vol. 3A). The Junction station is seen here in the 1950s, looking south towards Monmouth Road, with the line to the yard and branch diverging to the right.   R.F. ROBERTS/SLS

At the southern end of the Junction's triangular layout was a road overbridge carrying the B4233 Monmouth road (now A465) over the railway. The Abergavenny L&NW 0–8–0 just to the south of that bridge was banking the 7.50 a.m. Newquay to Manchester (London Road) express at the beginning of the 2½ mile section of 1 in 82, on Saturday, 18th September 1954. The train was usually of eleven coaches, but may have had more on this occasion to require the assisting engine. It was usual for such bankers on express passenger trains to remain uncoupled, and to ease off as it approached the summit at Llanvihangel.   RUSSELL MULFORD

NORTHERN APPROACHES TO ABERGAVENNY (Monmouth Road)

Halfway between the two stations, Firs Road crossed beneath the railway, although a public footbridge was provided over it. Worcester '43XX' 2–6–0 No.6388 is seen passing under the structure with a southbound special in the late morning of Friday, 9th July 1954.   R.F. ROBERTS/SLS

'County' No.1016 *County of Hants* running towards Monmouth Road station with a special in the late morning of Friday, 9th July 1954. The engine was allocated to Shrewsbury Coleham shed, and the train was almost certainly one from the North.   R.F. ROBERTS/SLS

Hereford Barton's 2-6-0 No.6352 is seen here passing the 22½ mile (22m 40c) milepost with a northbound class 'H' freight on Saturday, 18th September 1954. As with the great majority of goods trains on this route, it had probably originated in South Wales, conveying a head of mineral wagons.
RUSSELL MULFORD

Freight trains climbing up the 1 in 85 between Monmouth Road and Llanvihangel were mostly in need of banking, so that the train engine could take a heavier load over remaining, less-demanding sectors of its route by itself. Ex-L&NW 0-8-0s were frequently used from Monmouth Road in the 1950s, and one example is seen here banking the 2.5 p.m. Pengam to Saltney service on Saturday, 18th September 1954.
RUSSELL MULFORD

An ex-L&NW 0–8–0 is pictured here banking Chester's No.73038 with a Cardiff to Saltney train on Saturday, 18th September 1954. Abergavenny shed had seven of the class, though one was usually sufficient to cover the 4-mile (15–20 minute) banking runs to Llanvihangel. RUSSELL MULFORD

No.6849 *Walton Grange* heading under the footbridge with a West to North service on Saturday, 18th September 1954, the penultimate day of the summer programme. The engine was transferred from St. Philip's Marsh to Pontypool Road in October 1950, and took up both passenger and goods duties at the shed. Around summer 1954, Pontypool's 'Granges' were scheduled daily on parcels trains to and from Shrewsbury, and on the 4.40 p.m. Cardiff to Hereford passenger. They were also involved on one or two North & West expresses on summer Saturdays, and in particular the 8.15 a.m. Bristol to Manchester service, possibly the train seen here. During this month, the engine was transferred from Pontypool Road to Chester shed. RUSSELL MULFORD

Hereford '43XX' No.7301 starting away from Monmouth Road with a lightly-loaded class 'H' freight on Saturday, 18th September 1954. The '43XXs' could take 30 fully-loaded coal wagons (or other materials, contents 7 tons or over), 36 mineral (or other materials, less than 7 tons load) or 45 general merchandise – or a calculated mixture of the above – up the incline to Llanvihangel without assistance, a rather heavier weight than is being carried here. The north end of the Down Goods Loops connection off the Down Main is seen here on the left, serving a 48-wagon (plus engine & van) capacity on the outer loop, and 93 (or 50 to the Inner Home outlet) on the inner.

RUSSELL MULFORD

ABERGAVENNY MONMOUTH ROAD

Abergavenny (Monmouth Road) stands at 22m 63ch; it was the most important of the stations between Hereford and Pontypool Road and is still open for passengers. Monmouth Road handled Great Western passenger, goods shed and mileage traffic, whilst the Junction sidings dealt with the L&NW and LMS goods traffic. In the early days, Monmouth Road station was located at the extreme south-eastern edge of the town.

A drawing of the installation in 1880 shows the passenger facilities at the north end of the site, comprising an Up platform and a Down island platform. The line on the east face of the island platform was stopblocked at its north end, and was used for originating passenger traffic destined for Pontypool Road and beyond. Earlier, it had been a goods siding.

There was an engine shed on the Down side to the south of the island, used to house the banking engines for the incline to Llanfihangel, and for local main-line work. The single-road structure, of some 99ft in length, was built of stone, with a water tank, stores, and a coal platform adjacent. By 1901, this housed a '1076' class tank, a MR&C Goods 0-6-0ST and a pair of '3521' class 0-4-4Ts.

On the Up side, a goods shed stood to the south of the passenger station, with cattle pens and a dock to its northern side, and a three-road mileage yard to its south. A loading bank was situated on a spur from the outermost siding. There were two signal boxes, both on the Up side, a South box at the south end of the yard throat, and a North box off the south end of the Up platform.

At this time, there were no refuge facilities for goods trains between Llanvihangel and Pontypool Road, but in 1898 an Up Refuge Siding was provided at Monmouth Road; this was located to the south of the mileage yard, and held 34 wagons in addition to engine and brake. Around the Great War, the extended bay line that passed between the Down Main and the engine shed was nominated as a Down Refuge siding, housing a 45-wagon train in the Down direction, and 40 in the Up.

Diagrams of the early 1920s show the station with 323ft (Up) and 347ft (Down) platforms, and the bay of 350ft. Each platform had a water crane at its departure end, with the supply tank off the south end of the Down island platform.

The single-road shed was still in operation, now with a separate coal road at the rear, and a water crane at the south end to serve both the shed road and the adjacent Down Refuge Siding. At the Grouping, the shed housed one '645' and one '1076' class tank.

Adjacent to the south end of the Up platform, the cattle pen and loading dock accommodated three wagons, and was provided with a loading gauge. The 90ft goods shed held three 30 cwt cranes, and had a wagon weighbridge outside its south end, with a cart weighbridge in the roadway nearby. There was room for twelve wagons on the shed road, to its south.

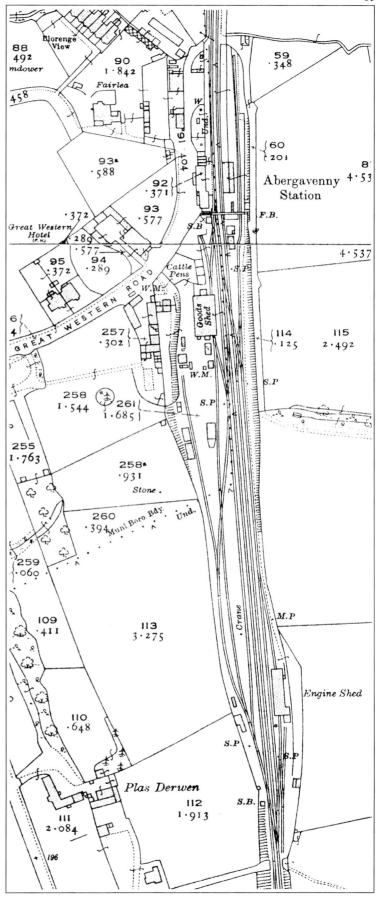

Taken from 25-inch Ordnance Survey for 1916. Crown Copyright reserved.

A variety of motive power was used on banking duties between Monmouth Road and Llanvihangel, much influenced by the change in ownership when the depot at Abergavenny closed, following which all the power was provided by Pontypool Road, who previously only provided part. Here Pontypool Road's 2–6–2T No.4130 was giving a much welcome push to a lengthy northbound mixed freight in 1950, the final year of her allocation at Pontypool Road, seen from the north end of the island platform. The former bay line and adjacent spur on the Down side were converted into two Goods Loops during late 1941, being extended northwards to connect with the Down Main, as seen here.

D.K JONES COLLECTION

No.73038 was from Chester shed, and was probably pictured with the 11.25 a.m. Pontypool Road to Saltney (SO) class 'H' service on a gloomy Saturday, 18th September 1954, its balancing duty off the Friday 10.45 a.m. Saltney to Stoke Gifford train. Scheduled for 'Standard Class 5' haulage, the train was timetabled for a five-minute call at Monmouth Road to attach the banker, which can be seen providing assistance at the rear.   RUSSELL MULFORD

The mileage yard comprised three loop sidings, with accommodation for 28, 14 and 9 wagons respectively (as from the Up Main), whilst a spur off the outer loop (third) held twenty more; the latter also served an 80ft wharf. A 5-ton yard crane was provided between the first and second loops, at their southern ends.

As before, the Refuge sidings were designated as 45 wagons (plus engine and brake) for the Down Refuge, though 40 when used as an Up Refuge. The Up Refuge, to the south of the South cabin, held a 34-wagon train.

In 1929, staff at Monmouth Road totalled 38:

Station Master	1
Booking Clerks	2
Booking & Parcel Clerk	1
Goods Clerks	6
Station Foreman	1
Ticket Collector	1
Parcel Porter	1
Porters	4
Goods Checkers	2
Goods Porters	3
Goods Shunters	4
Signalmen, North Box	3
South Box	3
Loading Carter	1
Goods Carters	3
Motor Driver	1
Charwoman (One day per wk.)	1

The station was not open for 24 hours. Its main work was carried out between 7 a.m. and 10 p.m., with a couple of Up trains between 4.0 and 6.10 a.m. probably dealt with by an early-turn porter – there would have been few passengers at that hour. The Foreman probably worked with the SM to cover the day between them as circumstances dictated, whilst the Ticket Collector was probably there only at peak passenger movement hours. There were also 4 porters, who would also be closely involved in station work.

In the following economy drives, staff numbers were reduced to 32 by 1934, with porters, shunters and a goods clerk removed from the establishment.

The engine shed at Monmouth Road closed in July 1932, and servicing of the main bank engine was transferred to Brecon Road LMS shed. In early 1932, Abergavenny shed housed one '1076' (No. 744) and one '2721' (No. 2749) class tank engines, with Taff Vale 'A' Class No. 385 arriving in March to see out the allocation.

The duties on the bank involved two Monmouth Road engines in early 1932, one from 11.15 p.m. to 9.30 p.m. the following day, and the other from 12.30 a.m. to 8.0 a.m. Following the closure of the shed, one GWR engine left Brecon Road shed at 1.20 a.m. to carry out shunting and banking for 14 hours. A Newport engine also spent a couple of hours banking from 3.0 a.m., whilst LMS engines covered the 4.0 p.m. to 1.40 a.m. duty.

Signalling arrangements were altered when the two signal boxes were closed in March 1934, and replaced by one new box on the Down side, opposite the goods yard.

In 1941, two Down Goods Loops were created, one formed by extending the island platform bay line northwards to a new connection out of the Down line, which held a 93-wagon-length train when added to the existing Down Refuge, or 50 on its own. The second loop was added alongside, to the outer side, and also accommodated engine, 50 wagons and brake. No. 1 loop (nearest to platform) could rejoin the main line just to the south of the platform, or at the south end of the complex along the old Down refuge, along with No. 2.

The goods shed was closed in 1966 and some of the yard connections also removed. In 1967, the Down Goods Loops were cut back to refuge sidings, and these were still in place with an Up Goods loop and signal box in 1976.

A '56XX' charged with banking what may well have been the 10.5 a.m. Penzance to Liverpool train one evening in the early 1950s, illustrating yet another engine type used on the duties. The freight on the right was standing on No.1 Down Goods Loop alongside the bay platform awaiting a clear road to Penpergwm or beyond. Also apparent on the Down platform in this view is a GWR type running-in board, and gas light standards, the nearer with the 'lozenge' style station nameplate attached below the light.

JOHN BEARDSMORE

No.5377 bringing her southbound class 'F' express freight (30 m.p.h. maximum) off the gradient at Monmouth Road in the mid-afternoon of Saturday, 18th September 1954. The engine was from Hereford (Barton) shed, and was probably hauling the 6.25 a.m. Annesley (ER) to Pontypool Road onwards from Coleham, to return on Monday morning with the 4.35 a.m. freight to Hereford.

RUSSELL MULFORD

Unrebuilt 'Patriot' No. 45520 *Llandudno* entrusted with the Longsight through working to Pontypool Road on the 9.10 a.m. Manchester to Swansea express, seen here coasting through the Down platform at Monmouth Road in the late 'fifties. It would return to Manchester with the 7.30 a.m. Penzance (7.50 Newquay on summer Saturdays), due back around 7.30 p.m. In winter months, the weekday 9.10 a.m. could be lightly loaded with as few as seven vehicles from Manchester and Birkenhead, but in summer with as many as thirteen regular coaches.
RALPH CHARLES

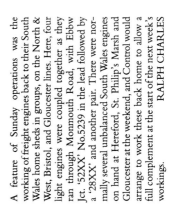

A feature of Sunday operations was the working of freight engines back to their South Wales home sheds in groups, on the North & West, Bristol, and Gloucester lines. Here, four light engines were coupled together as they ran through Monmouth Road, with Ebbw Jct. '52XX' No.5239 in the lead followed by a '28XX' and another pair. There were normally several unbalanced South Wales engines on hand at Hereford, St. Philip's Marsh and Gloucester at the weekend, and Control would arrange to work these back home to allow a full complement at the start of the next week's workings.
RALPH CHARLES

Looking south from the Up platform in the later 1950s, with a tank engine banker on the Down Main returning to base before performing another duty banking a freight, or perhaps even a passenger service. The station was on a level stretch of ground, and the heavy gradient to Llanvihangel started at the north end of the platforms with a section of 1 in 85 preceding the main climb of 1 in 82. To the left of the station, the footbridge extension can be seen to serve the footpath that ran southwards alongside the eastern edge of the line. The original gas lighting has been replaced by electric lamps on concrete posts, whilst the running-in boards are now of the enamel panel type.

R.K. BLENCOWE COLLECTION

An auto service standing at the Bay platform on Saturday, 8th July 1950 powered by Pontypool Road's '64XX' No.6430, with two auto cars. There was a daily 12.23 p.m. Pontypool Road to Abergavenny Monmouth Rd. passenger service at this time, but on Saturdays this was extended to run from Newport (departing 11.55 a.m.), though it was not specified for an auto. In the late 1950s, this duty was scheduled for auto trailers. The engine was in its final GWR livery, though with the addition of a smokebox numberplate. The original 'Abergavenny' running-in board can be seen immediately to the right of the engine on the Up platform, together with its recently-acquired 'Monmouth Road' appendage.

T.C. COLE

Pontypool Road '45XX' No. 4593 with the 11.45 a.m. Pontrilas to Pontypool Road local freight, arriving at Monmouth Road in 1958. This was the return of the 6.45 a.m. Pontypool Road to Pontrilas local freight, which called at Monmouth Road between 12.38 and 1.28 p.m., and is pictured on the Goods Loop alongside the bay platform. By this time, most of the traffic was mileage, reflected in the number of mineral wagons on the train.   D.K. JONES COLLECTION

Monmouth Road station towards the end of the steam era, looking south from the edge of the bay platform in the late morning of Tuesday, 19th May 1964; the line serving the 350ft bay originally stood alone here, terminating by a stop block at the north end. The banker on this occasion was Pontypool Road '72XX' 2–8–2T No.7220, seen standing on the outer (No.2) Down Goods Loop to the south of the footbridge. Beyond the awning of the Down shelter, No.9475 (nominally from Neath at this time) was shunting alongside the goods shed. The barrow crossing at the south end of the platforms can be seen here extending to the east side of the line, connecting via a ramp to a gateway, whilst a number of trolleys can be seen around the station, probably indicating a fairly healthy parcels traffic.

MICHAEL HALE /GW TRUST

In terms of faster trains, Monmouth Road station was mostly served by the Cardiff & Birmingham services, with around four each way daily. Of these, the 9.50 a.m. Cardiff to Birmingham was usually powered by a Canton Standard 'Class 4', the shed having four such engines allocated following the withdrawal of the 'Saints'. It ran to Hereford with this train, and returned with the 3.10 p.m. (12.45 p.m. Snow Hill SX) or the 4.10 p.m. on Saturdays, then carried out a return trip to Swansea in the evening. The formation was a seven-coach set, increased to ten on Saturdays, returning as the 5.0 p.m. from Snow Hill. Here, No. 75007 is seen easing into Monmouth Road with the 9.50, with the fireman preparing the engine for the Llanvihangel climb.
RALPH CHARLES

The empty stock of the SLS special carrying out the final passenger run over the MT&A line on 5th January 1958 is seen here at Monmouth Road's Down platform behind one of the engines involved. Abergavenny-based '7F' 0–8–0 No.49121. The engine was carrying a headboard declaring 'Last Train Ebbw Vale & Rhymney Branches', and was fitted with a BR smokebox shed code ('86K', formerly LMS '4D'), but no number plate. This was probably the ECS coming down from Abergavenny Junction to start the train from Monmouth Road, whilst its passengers waited on the Up platform.
R.K. BLENCOWE COLLECTION

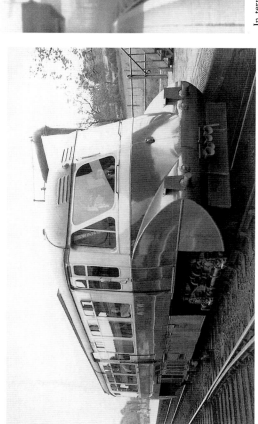

Diesel Railcar No.11 spent the early 1950s at Landore, and was transferred to Worcester during 1956 for its final years of service. The car is seen here standing at the south end of the Down platform, Monmouth Road, on an unknown service in the early 1950s, but appears to have been awaiting departure for the south. Perhaps it was on loan to Newport or Pontypool Road at the time, and was working one of the Abergavenny local turns.
COLLECTION D.K. JONES

Very few N&W expresses called at Abergavenny (Monmouth Road) in GWR or early BR(W) days, but by the early 1960s the number of these increased, as local services had been removed with the closure of the smaller stations on the line. From Monmouth Road they faced a tough uphill start, and were often banked to Llanvihangel at the rear. Here, the 11.0 a.m. Plymouth to Manchester was calling at Abergavenny on Thursday, 5th September 1963, where Pontypool Road's 2–8–2T No.7206 had buffered up to assist up the bank, with the guard going to check details with the driver. The agricultural importance of the area is highlighted by stock sale notices on the right.

BJ. ASHWORTH

Ex-Taff Vale class 'A' 0–6–2T No.385, one of two such engines allocated to Pontypool Road at the time (the other being No.349), standing on No.2 Down Goods Loop near the footbridge at the south end of Monmouth Road station on 6th July 1950. These engines were often used as bankers, and No.385 had probably just returned from a trip up the bank; it was now awaiting its next task. Although it had received its smokebox number, the engine was not yet carrying a shed code plate, which came a little later in the nationalisation process (from late 1949).

T.C. COLE

Abergavenny Monmouth Road station seen from the goods shed siding in July 1964, looking towards Hereford, with the main building on the left (Up) side and the shelter on the right (Down), the platforms connected by the footbridge. The water crane on the Down platform is also evident in this view, served (along with those on the Up platform and in the yards) by the tank on the right.

T.C. COLE

Coleham 'Castle' No.5073 *Blenheim* leaving Monmouth Road in the mid-1950s with a southbound train. It is possible that this was the Sunday 2.0 p.m. Shrewsbury to Newport, a semi-fast service, the engine of which returned from Newport with the 5.40 p.m. Bristol to Crewe, one of the few N&W services to call at Newport, detach Cardiff coaches, then reverse out to continue its journey.   RALPH CHARLES

Shrewsbury 'County' No.1022 *County of Northampton* pausing at Monmouth Road with the 3.50 p.m. Shrewsbury to Cardiff service in 1963. The train was carrying an 'A' headcode, as the local ('B') services no longer existed on the N&W, with only the principal and main intermediate stations surviving; Monmouth Road was now the only call between Hereford and Pontypool Road. The rugged stonework on the supporting structure for the water tower is very evident here.   J. BEARDSMORE

Running past the goods shed en route to performing another banking duty, Abergavenny-based 0-8-0 No. 49403 was lit by the afternoon sun in this rare view of activities at Monmouth Road, taken on Saturday, 24th August 1957, looking south from the Up platform. In addition to the goods shed on the right, the water tower, cabin, and the 1934 replacement timber signal box are seen to the left, with the old engine shed beyond in the distance. Above the engine, the starting signal was still branded 'Bay', even though the two lines beyond it were nominally Goods Loops.
IAN L. WRIGHT

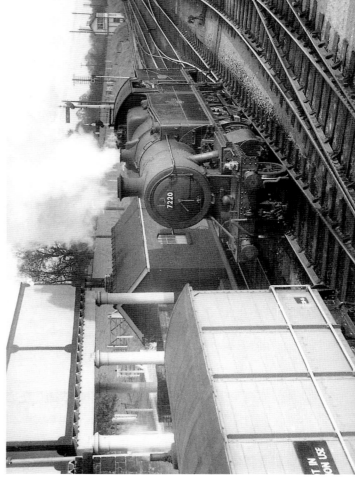

Pontypool Road's No.7220 is seen here running forward on the Up Main to buffer up to a northbound freight for the 4-mile climb to Llanvihangel in the later 1950s. Transferred to Pontypool Road in 1954, the engine's freight duties alternated with periodic banking turns; in use, it was frequently more powerful than the train engine it was assisting.
J. BEARDSMORE

Llanelly '43XX' No.7307 heading north with a class 'H' freight in the mid-afternoon of Wednesday, 14th August 1957. The train was probably the 7.15 a.m. Llanelly (Llandilo Jct.) to Hereford (Worcester Sidings), which ran via the Swansea District and Vale of Neath routes, and was due to pass Monmouth Road at 4.11 p.m. It contains a good proportion of mineral and metal-carrying wagons, with just a handful of vans, conveyed through from Llandilo Jct., Felin Fran and Neath Jct. The engine turn was LLY 5, a '43XX' duty which took it as far north as Coleham.　　B.K.B. GREEN/
INITIAL PHOTOGRAPHICS

Pontypool Road's No.7220 is seen standing on No.2 Down Goods Loop on Tuesday, 19th May 1964, awaiting her next banking duty. The water tank seen above the cab provided some of the station supply, including the water cranes at the departure end of each main platform, and those serving the exit ends of the Up and Down Goods Loops. By its position, the cabin to the left of the engine was possibly used by enginemen.　　MICHAEL HALE

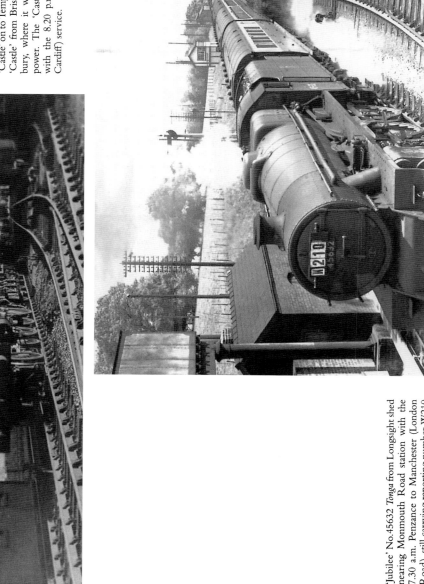

Highlighted in the early evening sun, the 10.5 a.m. Penzance to Liverpool train approaching Monmouth Road behind an unidentified 'Castle', probably from Bath Road shed, in the early 1950s. The headcode '660' was carried by the service from 1946 to 1954, and became '285' in 1955. In the winter 1953 schedule, engine power for this train involved a Penzance 'Hall' to Plymouth; a Newton or Bath Road 'Castle' on to Temple Meads; and a Bath Road 'Castle' from Bristol (4.30 p.m.) to Shrewsbury, where it was handed over to LMR power. The 'Castle' returned that evening with the 8.20 p.m. Crewe to Bristol (and Cardiff) service.   RALPH CHARLES

'Jubilee' No.45632 *Tonga* from Longsight shed nearing Monmouth Road station with the 7.30 a.m. Penzance to Manchester (London Road), still carrying reporting number W210 from the down journey on the 9.15 a.m. Manchester to Swansea, which it had worked as far as Pontypool Road. The '7F' was waiting in the adjacent siding for its next banking turn.
D.S. FISH

Canton Standard 'Class 4' No.75009 running into Monmouth Road with the 2.45 p.m. stopper from Cardiff to Hereford, scheduled for a four corridor coach set in the mid-1950s. There were five such coach sets (from Newport Ebbw carriage shed) running a five-day cycle between them that covered 15 different trains; on the 'fourth' day, the 2.45 p.m. Cardiff was one set's only working. The Canton engine was on its second scheduled Cardiff to Hereford return trip of the day, and would finally return to Cardiff with the 7.12 p.m. Hereford (5.0 p.m. Birmingham) service. LMR '3P' 2–6–2T No.40145 was awaiting its next banking turn in the siding alongside the goods shed.

JOHN BEARDSMORE

The goods shed, cattle pens and loading dock can be seen with a horse box on the extreme right in this view of Worcester 'Star' No.4051 *Princess Helena* passing with a West to North service on Saturday, 8th July 1950. The express, with reporting number '573', was the Saturdays-only 8.15 a.m. Paignton to Manchester (Victoria), due through Abergavenny at 12.45 p.m.; it was scheduled for ten LMR coaches, and contained some interesting former LMS stock behind the tender. No.4051 was mostly utilised to the London side of Hereford, and has probably been borrowed for this turn; she was condemned three months later.
T.C. COLE

A detailed view of the goods shed, doubtless the original stone building, with Pontypool Road 'Pannier' No.3717 shunting for the day on 4th July 1959. The shed was probably being additionally used for full wagon traffic, with sacks on the deck alongside a van. In the middle distance, further along the yard, a couple more vans are seen alongside the raised agricultural warehouse, in which sliding doors gave direct access to the interior. The yard's mileage sidings are visible in the distance, on the right.
F.K. DAVIES/
GREAT WESTERN TRUST

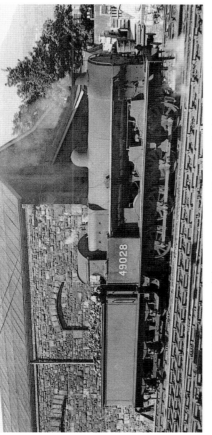

Webb 'Coal Tank' No.7752 (soon to be No.58913) from Abergavenny is seen on the goods shed siding alongside Monmouth Road's main building in the late morning of Friday, 16th September 1949. It was probably on a transfer turn from and to Junction station, one of the 'LMR engines for shunting and banking as required' specified in the Service Timetable.
R.J. BUCKLEY/INITIAL PHOTOGRAPHICS

Ex-L&NW '7F' No.49028 of Abergavenny shed awaiting its next banking duty on the siding alongside the goods shed c.1951, with the fireman building up steam. Examples of the class remained at Abergavenny (Union Road) shed until its closure in 4th January 1958, by which time the great majority in the area were in 'Store' awaiting the condemnation order, though a couple worked on briefly from Pontypool Road.
R.J. BUCKLEY/INITIAL PHOTOGRAPHICS

Pontypool Road also used lighter engines for its banking duties, evidenced by '45XX' No.4541, standing on the No.2 Down Goods Loop on 16th September 1949. The engine was still carrying its final GWR livery, with the shed code on the frame behind the buffer beams. '45XXs' at the shed were known to work Vale of Neath freights, and on passenger services to Aberdare. No.4541 had been at Pontypool Road since 1947, and would move into West Wales in autumn 1952. The agricultural warehouse in the goods yard behind the engine was a familiar sight at rural stations, mostly used for storing and distributing such supplies, in this case by the Bibby company. R.J. BUCKLEY/INITIAL PHOTOGRAPHICS

Looking northwards from the headshunt spur at the south end of Monmouth Road goods yard on 25th September 1952; at the near end of the yard can be seen a loading gauge (left) and the yard crane (right) . The Up Goods Loop, converted from the Refuge Siding in 1941, was behind the photographer, just beyond the headshunt stopblock. To the right can be seen the ruins of the old engine shed, which was situated on a short loop off the Down Goods Loop, with its own pair of short sidings at the near end. A water crane remained at the near end, together with the water tank that supplied it. The bracket signals on the right controlled the Down Main and the Goods Loop exit respectively. In the middle distance, in the centre of the picture, a '72XX' can be seen on the Down Goods Loop awaiting its next banking turn.

PENPERGWM

'28XX' class 2–8–0 No.3812 rolling past the bracket signal near the entrance to the Down Goods Running Loop at Penpergwm one evening, c.1954. The engine was from Canton shed, and the train may have been one of the early-afternoon departures from Shrewsbury (Coton Hill or Coleham) to Pontypool Road. The composition was typical, with a good selection of mineral wagons, a few vans and one or two bogie vehicles.   D.S. FISH

The station at Penpergwm (25m 38ch) stood alongside the A40 trunk road some $2\frac{3}{4}$ miles to the south of Abergavenny, close to the hamlet after which it was named.

An 1880 drawing shows two equal length platforms with a level crossing at the south end. A signal box was located on the Up side, to the north of the platform, facing the connections into the small, single loop mileage yard, with a cattle pen on its southern spur.

A Down Refuge siding accommodating 45 wagons (plus engine and brake) had been added at the north end of the site by 1921, at which time the station was recorded with a Down platform giving a nominal 198ft (though it was longer), and a 348ft Up platform. The mileage siding accommodated 21 vehicles, and a spur off its south end ran behind the Down platform to serve a 'loading platform' of 190ft, this dimension perhaps reducing the effective length of platform serving the

Canton 'Britannia' No.70023 *Venus* approaching the site of the northern end of Penpergwm's Refuge Loop, to the north of the station, with a Down express in the afternoon of a bright winter's day in the late 1950s. The engine was on one of the three daytime Canton turns that ran to and from Shrewsbury, and this was probably the returning 2.24 p.m. from Shrewsbury to Bristol, the 11.45 a.m. Manchester to Plymouth service. The goods loop was taken out of service around this time, and the home arm had been removed from the bracket.
                                                                JOHN BEARDSMORE

These views show a short Down class 'J' freight in the Goods Running Loop at Penpergwm during an afternoon in the mid-1950s. The train was doubled-headed by a pair of tank engines, with the train engine 2–8–2T No.7204 and assistant engine '51XX' No.4138, both from Pontypool Road. The '51XX' was probably returning to shed on a 'RAO' (return as ordered) leg, possibly having worked the passenger or mail from Newport to Abergavenny (Monmouth Road); it was common to attach unbalanced engines to a train rather than run light engine, as its power could be used to good effect, and it avoided taking up an individual path over that often busy part of the route.

JOHN BEARDSMORE

Down Main. Cattle pens were located on the outer side of this line. A short spur at the north end of the mileage siding held two wagons.

Staff in the interwar period totalled five, with the stationmaster supervising two porters and two signalmen. The box was open between 6.0 a.m. and 10.0 p.m., thereafter being switched out, with Abergavenny South and Nantyderry taking the section on weekday nights.

The Down Refuge siding was extended back northwards in 1941 to become a Down Running Loop, with a capacity of engine, 65 wagons and a brake.

In June 1958, the station was closed for passenger and goods traffic. All connections and sidings were recovered in 1959, and the signal box closed and dismantled in 1964.

Overtaking a southbound freight standing in the down goods running loop, Newton Abbot 'Castle' No.4077 *Chepstow Castle* is seen here approaching Penpergwm with a North to West express on Saturday, 8th July 1950. The train, with rather oddly numbered plates displaying '240', was the Saturdays-only 8.50 a.m. Liverpool to Penzance, with the rear portion containing coaches from Birkenhead (9.5 a.m.) to Penzance and to Kingswear.   T.C. COLE/ G.W. SHARPE COLLECTION

Britannia No.70028 *Royal Star* approaching Penpergwm with a Down express in an early evening c.1954, passing the exit end of the goods running loop, which was still extant at the time. The train was probably the 3.0 p.m. Liverpool to Cardiff service, with seven (or so) coaches, the return working for the Canton engine of the 11.15 a.m. Swansea to Manchester.   D.S. FISH

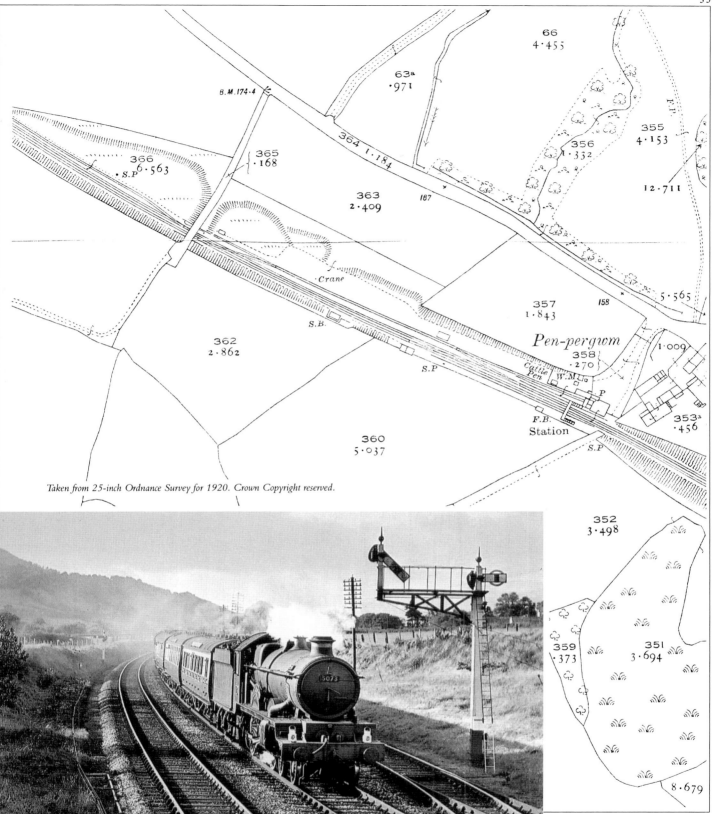

Taken from 25-inch Ordnance Survey for 1920. Crown Copyright reserved.

During a mid-afternoon in the mid-1950s, Shrewsbury 'Castle' No.5073 *Blenheim* heading past the Down Loop on the approach to Penpergwm with what was probably the 11.55 a.m. Manchester to the West Country service. The majority of 'Castles' on the route daily were from Coleham, Canton, Bath Road and Newton Abbot sheds, with occasional visits from Laira.

Heading south through Penpergwm station in 1952, Shrewsbury 'County' No.1018 *County of Leicester* is seen with the 11.55 a.m. Manchester to Plymouth, which also conveyed a portion for Paignton at the rear. The engine worked as far as Temple Meads with this train. The local goods facilities at Penpergwm, seen behind the train, consisted of a single siding with a trailing connection to the main at each end, giving a headshunt (2-wagon capacity), a mileage siding (21 wagons) and another spur (10 wagons) originally with a 5-ton crane, a loading bank and cattle pens, by this time largely disused.

J.G. HUBBACK/AUTHOR'S COLLECTION

No.2892 running past a freshly-painted name-board on the Down platform at Penpergwm with a class 'F' freight in the 1950s. The engine was at Canton until early 1959, when she was moved to Severn Tunnel Jct. The loading dock can be seen behind the railings, though doubt-less little used by this time.

JOHN BEARDSMORE

'Castle' No.5053 *Earl Cairns* of Newton Abbot shed nearing the level crossing at the south end of Penpergwm station with train No.274, at 3.40 p.m. on Saturday, 17th May 1958. This service was probably a relief to the 7.30 a.m. Penzance to Manchester (No.273). Newton shed had a daily turn to Shrewsbury, alternating with Coleham shed, but also operated a further three (or so) Friday night/Saturday trains from the Torbay line over the N&W route. The road across the tracks seen here was little more than a farm track, but access had nevertheless to be provided, and at Penpergwm the arrangement was a combined barrow and road crossing made of sleepering.   JOHN BEARDSMORE

Canton 'Hall' No.5946 *Marwell Hall*, easing into the Up platform with the 2.45 p.m. Cardiff to Hereford during November 1955. The 2.45 p.m. called at Marshfield, Newport, Pontypool Road and all stations to Hereford (except St. Devereux), and was formed of the 'classic' four-coach corridor rake (Van Third, Third, Compo, Van Third) with, in this instance, a strengthening Third at the head. There were five such sets working on a cycle of duties in the area, which took each formation as far afield as Carmarthen, Cheltenham and Shrewsbury in turn during the five days. The church tower at Llangattock-nigh-Usk can be seen in the distance.   JOHN BEARDSMORE

LLANVAIR BRIDGE

The Shrewsbury double-home turn to Newton Abbot was worked by low-mileage, recently ex-works 'Castles' and 'Counties' from Coleham and by 'Castles' from Newton, though while they still had a 'Britannia' (No.70022 *Tornado*) this was sometimes utilised. Here, an immaculate Shrewsbury 'County' No. 1003 *County of Wilts* was climbing Nantyderry bank just to the north of the road bridge with the 9.10 a.m. Liverpool to Plymouth on Friday, 7th March 1958. Although she looks ex-works, she was actually now four months out of Swindon, a tribute to the depot's presentation skills. The six-coach Liverpool to Plymouth portion (with Dining Car) was at the head of the train, and the three-coach Manchester to Kingswear at the rear.
R.O. TUCK

With Skirrid Fach discernible in the background, Cardiff East Dock 'Hall' No. 6918 *Sandon Hall* is seen on the ascent of the bank with the 10.42 a.m. Llandudno to Cardiff (1V56) on Saturday, 24th August 1963. This was the return working of the 8.20 a.m. Cardiff to Llandudno, which the engine worked to Shrewsbury. BR standard coaching stock now formed much of the express trains on the route, although some examples from the pre-Nationalization era were still common, especially on Saturdays.
R.O. TUCK

The most interesting working of the day for enthusiasts and photographers in the area was the through working of the Longsight engine on the 9.25 a.m. Manchester London Road to Swansea as far as Pontypool Road, returning in under two hours with the 7.30 a.m. Penzance to Manchester. The power provided could be a 'Royal Scot', unrebuilt or rebuilt 'Patriot', or 'Jubilee', and here on 7th March 1958 unrebuilt 'Patriot' No.45519 *Lady Godiva* is seen with the Down working, passing Nantyderry Down Distant on the 1 in 80 climb of Nantyderry bank, a few miles north of Pontypool Road. A smart turn-round was involved at Pontypool off the Down working – which arrived at 1.25 p.m. – to come back off shed after servicing by 3.0 p.m. for the 3.19 p.m. return, with the tender topped up with best Welsh steam coal, although the Midlands/Northern coal being burned here by the Patriot was producing a fine white exhaust.

R.O. TUCK

Nothing more powerful than this ageing and grimy Mogul No.5313 was provided by Shrewsbury depot on Saturday, 14th September 1957 for the heavy 9.5 a.m. Birkenhead to Plymouth and Cardiff (reporting number 216), again seen climbing Nantyderry bank. The train would divide at Pontypool Road, the train engine probably working to Cardiff. Judging by the black exhaust, the fireman was still working hard with his shovel. A mixture of trackwork design can be seen in these views, with traditional 'Bullhead' and chairs in use on the Down Main, and flat-bottomed on the Up.   R.O. TUCK

Veteran Pontypool Road '28XX' No.2802 climbing Nantyderry bank in the southbound direction on 14th September 1957 with a Class 'H' freight that could have run as a a much higher category, given the amount of vacuum next to the engine. Forty years earlier, this was one of the engines involved in working the 'Jellicoe Specials' over this route taking coal from the Aberdare and Rhondda pits to the fleet at Scapa Flow in the 1914 War, Pontypool Road engines and men working through to Chester/Warrington. No.2802 was recorded in incidents with these trains during 1916/17, when she would still have had inside steampipes and a straight front end.   R.O. TUCK

Newton Abbot 'Castle' No.5059 *Earl St. Aldwyn* returning west with the 9.10 a.m. Manchester (London Road) to Plymouth – a heavy train of thirteen or so coaches on the day – on the return leg of her double-home working on Saturday, 10th August 1957. She was working hard on the final stage of the 1 in 80 Nantyderry bank, passing under the three-arch bridge near Llanvair. The crew were normally from Newton too, also working home, and would hand over the train to a fresh engine and crew there for the final leg to North Road.

R.O. TUCK

Framed by the bridge, Canton 'Modified Hall' No.6963 *Throwley Hall* climbing Nantyderry bank with the 8.45 a.m. (SO) Liverpool to Penzance on Saturday, 10th August 1957. This train left Shrewsbury at 10.52 a.m., and was usually worked by a Chester 'Hall' as far as Bristol, but doubtless one of Canton's night-time turns to Shrewsbury had been called upon to fill a gap in motive power; the Chester shed turn ended up at Cardiff on Saturday nights in any event.

R.O. TUCK

The nine-coach 9.15 a.m. Manchester to Swansea climbing up Nantyderry bank behind Longsight 'Royal Scot' No.46163 *Civil Service Rifleman* on Saturday, 17th February 1962. This view, taken from the top of the cutting, shows the depth of the earthworks, and the consequent height and length of the road span across it. Llanvair Grange was situated a short distance to the right of the bungalows seen on the right.
R.O. TUCK

Crewe North 'Royal Scot' No. 46125 *3rd Carabinier* was provided for the through working to Pontypool Road on Saturday, 4th August 1962, and is seen at the top of the 1 in 80 climb from Penpergwm with the 9.30 a.m. Liverpool to Plymouth. The 'Scots' were effectively the equivalent of the more powerful of the Western Region 4-6-0s, although their tractive effort was slightly greater than either 'Castle' or 'County'; as with that pair – and the 'Britannias' – the 'Royal Scots' (along with the rebuilt 'Patriots') were limited to a 455-ton maximum load over the route from Shrewsbury to Pontypool Road, though 420 tons from Pontypool Road back to Hereford.
R.O. TUCK

Stanier '8F' 2–8–0s were a common sight along the North & West, particularly in the final years of steam haulage, and here Shrewsbury's No.48735 was heading south with a class '6' ('E') partly fitted freight (with 'not less than four braked vehicles connected by vacuum pipe to the engine') on Saturday, 8th August 1964, probably bound for Cardiff judging by the empty banana vans in the front part of the train, and eventually destined for Barry Docks for reloading from an inwards Geest vessel from the West Indies. The change in period can be seen by the colour light Down Distant in place of the former semaphore signal, beyond the tall bridge carrying the Croes Llanvair to Pen-groes-oped (etc.) country lane.

R.O. TUCK

With the bridge in the background, this classic view is enhanced by Canton 'Castle' No.4080 *Powderham Castle* at the head of the 9.30 a.m. Manchester to Swansea, which the engine worked through from Shrewsbury to Cardiff on Saturday, 4th August 1962. The engine had just entered the gentle S-bend that took the line into Nantyderry station on gentle gradiens. R.O. TUCK

From 9th September 1960, 'Kings' – now allocated to Cardiff Canton – reappeared on the North & West after a gap of some 8–10 years since Nos.6000/18 were transferred away from Bristol. The Canton 'Kings' often worked the 8.55 a.m., 1.13 p.m. and 7.20 p.m. Cardiff to Shrewsbury turns, though priority was given to coverage of the three Canton turns to London. Here, No.6023 *King Edward II* was returning from Shrewsbury with the 12.15 p.m. Manchester to Plymouth, climbing Nantyderry bank on a working through to Bristol on 19th May 1962, the last week of 'King' operation at the depot. R.O. TUCK

Canton 'Castle' No.5021 *Whittington Castle* returning south from Shrewsbury with the 9.30 a.m. Manchester to Swansea (the 'V54' displayed on a rather frugal LMR board) on Saturday, 1st September 1962, having just climbed the bank. Trains between the North of England and South Wales were fewer in number than the West Country services, but still carried fairly heavy loads, with the 9.30 scheduled for seven to Swansea and six to Cardiff. Only twenty days later, at the end of the Summer service, the engine was withdrawn from traffic and was eventually sold as scrap to John Cashmore of Newport Town Dock.   R.O. TUCK

This Class 6 ('E') Down partly-fitted freight from either Chester or Shrewsbury to South Wales reaching the top of Nantyderry bank behind Pontypool Road 2–8–0 No. 3859 on Saturday, 1st September 1962. As befitting its 'express' class, the visible section of the train comprised general merchandise wagons, with little or no mineral traffic on board. The train was limited to a maximum speed of 35 mph, with between four and eleven (minimum, depending upon length) and half the total number of wagons (maximum) connected by vacuum to the engine.   R.O. TUCK

On Saturday, 1st September 1962, the LMR working to Pontypool Road was double-headed, presumably as the train in one or both directions was overweight for the train engine. Shrewsbury Class '5' No.45298 with self-weighing tender was piloting Crewe North's rebuilt 'Patriot' No. 45545 *Planet*, the pair seen here having just climbed Nantyderry bank and with power now mostly shut off to coast along the gentle gradient towards Nantyderry en route to Pontypool Road, where they would leave the train.   R.O. TUCK

Returning north the same day, the pair are seen at the head of the 10.45 a.m. Kingswear to Manchester, coasting down the 1 in 80 on Nantyderry bank.

R.O. TUCK

A view from the Llanvair bridge looking down onto the North & West line, showing Shrewsbury 'County' No. 1016 *County of Hants* coasting down Nantyderry bank as it returned north on the double-home working with the 8.0 a.m. (Saturdays excepted) Plymouth to Liverpool on Thursday, 8th August 1957. In the week following the August Bank Holiday, traffic would still have been heavy, and the train had at least one coach over the scheduled twelve. This service carried a multitude of sections, from Plymouth to Glasgow, Liverpool and Manchester, and from Kingswear to Manchester.   R.O. TUCK

A Class ('Black') '5' was all that Crewe North could provide for the through run to Pontypool Road on Saturday, 24th August 1963, by when one would have thought that Class '6' and '7' power was more plentiful. No. 44678 is seen approaching the top of the bank with the 10.15 a.m. Plymouth to Manchester, for which M95 had been expertly etched on the smokebox. The train appears to have had a load of around twelve, approaching its published limit for the climb from Abergavenny to Llanvihangel unassisted.   R.O. TUCK

Double heading sometimes took place on the North & West, either to rectify a power imbalance or to provide for an overloaded train. In this view of the 1M95, the 10.15 a.m. Plymouth to Manchester, Cardiff East Dock 'Modified Hall' No.7913 *Little Wyrley Hall* was piloting Neath Hall No.5972 *Olton Hall* as they began the descent of the 1 in 80 incline towards Penpergwm on Saturday, 21st July 1962. A contrast of Collett (No.2393) and Hawksworth (No.4100) tenders may be seen on the engines.

R.O. TUCK

Looking south towards Nantyderry, with Shrewsbury 'County' No. 1022 *County of Northampton* heading the 11.0 a.m. Exeter to Manchester on Saturday, 21st July 1962. Three months later this engine was withdrawn. The 10.0 a.m. Exeter ran during the peak of the summer Saturday timetable only, and formed a relief to the following 9.5 a.m. Paignton, although it was overtaken by that Torbay service (which ran via the main line) as the 10.0 a.m. made a quite lengthy call at Weston-super-Mare. The train usually carried the 'M90' code, the first numeral of which appears to be missing in this instance. The leading coach was an ex-LNER Gresley vehicle, perhaps the most distinctive design of the four old companies.
R.O. TUCK

The returning LMR Crewe North Summer Saturday working to Pontypool Road, with 'Jubilee' No. 45567 *South Australia* coasting down the bank with the 10.45 a.m. Kingswear to Liverpool on 21st July 1962. This train traditionally carried a Kingswear to Manchester portion at the head, and a Paignton to Liverpool at the rear. It was the third of four regular Saturday morning trains running from Torbay to Manchester via the N&W during the summer timetable at this time.
R.O. TUCK

LMR 'Britannias' became more common on the through working to Pontypool Road on Saturdays, when the engine was provided by Crewe North during the last years of steam haulage over the line. No.70054 *Dornoch Firth* is pictured with the Saturdays-only service '1M93', the 10.20 a.m. Kingswear to Manchester Piccadilly, running northwards on the 1 in 80 descent of Nantyderry bank on Saturday, 24th August 1963. As its name suggests, this was one of the five 'Firths' working in Scotland [from Polmadie (Glasgow) shed] during their early days, and later in No.70054's case, from Leeds. R.O. TUCK

Shrewsbury Stanier '8F' No.48471 heading north from Nantyderry with an up Class '8' ('H') freight on Saturday, 1st September 1962, probably originating at Cardiff as the train had a good vacuum head of banana traffic from Barry Docks, loaded in containers. At this time, Coleham shed housed twelve of the engines, and their work included duties over both the North & West and the Central Wales (via Llandovery) into the Principality. R.O. TUCK

52

2·445

537
2·921

S.P

55
568

294

M.P

S.P

556
2·261

276

558
1·703

554
·989

Rectory

S.P

559
8·570

267

560
·268

48ª
3

F.B

S.P

B.M 261·0

552
3·253

S.P

Station

Nant-y-derry

3ᵇ
4

264

561
2·889

P.H

P.O

S.B

562
·458

23i

551
3·758

561ª
·858

Goytre

Nant-y-derry
House

578
3·877

571
3·390

580
3·111

579
·455

580ª
·184

Sl

Hydraulic Ram

576
2·777

S.P

572
12·513

581
2·472

575
1·925

S.P

F.B

Sl.

Spring

596
·945

Mill Race

Sl.

Robwl

589
4·415

Taken from 25-inch Ordnance Survey for 1920. Crown Copyright reserved.

NANTYDERRY (For GOYTRE)

Seen from the road bridge, Shrewsbury 'Hall' No.5958 *Knolton Hall*, with a Hawksworth tender, heading away north after a call with the 2.45 p.m. Cardiff to Hereford local train on Saturday, 17th May 1958, shortly before the station's closure. A timber waiting shelter was provided on the Down platform to afford welcome protection against the elements, no longer conveniently provided by the station building to the south of the bridge.   JOHN BEARDSMORE

Nantyderry station stood at 28m 6ch, just to the south of the road overbridge carrying the lane from Chain Bridge to Goytre. The station stood about a mile to the south of the summit of Nantyderry bank, which rose for about a mile at 1 in 80 in the Down direction before easing off to pass through the site.

An 1880 drawing shows two platforms of equal length on a curve, with a small, two-loop mileage yard with cattle pens on the Down side, south of the platform. The signal box was set back between the Down platform and the goods yard, and was renewed in 1912.

The early 1920s diagrams show the station with a 510ft Down platform, some two-thirds of which faced against the Down Main, with the remainder curving around the northern side of the yard trackwork. The Up platform was recorded as 386ft in length.

There were just two loop sidings shown, the innermost a storage siding with accommodation for 8 wagons, and the outer a mileage siding of the same capacity.

Nantyderry had seven staff in the 1920s/30s: the station-master, two porters, three signalmen and a lampman.

Passenger and goods facilities were withdrawn in 1958, with all connections and sidings recovered in 1959. The signal box closed and was dismantled in 1980 with further MAS coverage.

In its later guise, Nantyderry station had a staggered platform arrangement, with the Down platform to the north of the road bridge, and the Up on the south side, with the main station building also to the south of the bridge. This view looks south along the Down platform, with the road between Nantyderry and Goytre carried by the bridge. The main station building, was reached under the left-hand archway. The embankment to the right had been pinned back by a small retaining wall.   LENS OF SUTTON

Hereford Barton 'Hall' No.5977 *Beckford Hall* passing through Nantyderry c.1957 with a Down express. This may have been a Birmingham to Cardiff train, for which Barton shed provided some engines onwards from Hereford. This photograph also provides a good view of the old station building, now with its platform fenced off and isolated from the trains calling at the station. On the extreme left, to the left of the starting signal, can be seen the steps connecting the Up platform with the road bridge.　　JOHN BEARDSMORE

Newton Abbot 'Castle' No.5011 *Tintagel Castle* rounding the bend through Nantyderry station with the 8.0 a.m. Plymouth to Liverpool on Friday, 22nd March 1957. At this time, No.5011 was four months out of Swindon after a Heavy Intermediate overhaul, which had lasted from March until November 1956. The train carried the '263' headcode on weekdays between Plymouth (North Road) and Shrewsbury, and conveyed coaches from Plymouth to Liverpool (including Restaurant Car) and Glasgow, and Kingswear to Manchester, the latter attached to the rear of the train at Newton at the same time as the 'Castle' was attached to the front.

R.O. TUCK

A 'Hall' is pictured with an Up class 'H' mixed freight at Nantyderry in the later 1950s, with the load containing the usual selection of mineral wagons. The modest goods yard to the left now only had a single (formerly mileage) siding, the storage siding between it and the Down Main having been lifted.   JOHN BEARDSMORE

Here running through Nantyderry station, on its return from Wolverhampton Works for overhaul, we see Aberdare's '84XX' class 0–6–0PT No.8445, on 17th May 1958. The station building and signal box are seen to the right on the Down platform stub, with the steps leading up to the roadway behind the engine; the latter footbridge was believed to have been installed in June 1890 using 'labour by Company's men and materials from Stores'.   JOHN BEARDSMORE

Nantyderry signal box, signalman and station staff on Saturday, 17th May 1958. The box contained a 26-lever frame by this time to control the signals and points on the main line and in the small yard. JOHN BEARDSMORE

Another view of Shrewsbury 'Hall' No.5958 *Knolton Hall*, this time arriving at the Up platform with the four-coach 2.45 p.m. Cardiff to Hereford stopper on Saturday, 17th May 1958. The southernmost part of the station building can be seen on the left, with the signal box immediately beyond, and the small goods yard to its far side. Distinctive 'swan-neck' lamps provide illumination on the platform.
JOHN BEARDSMORE

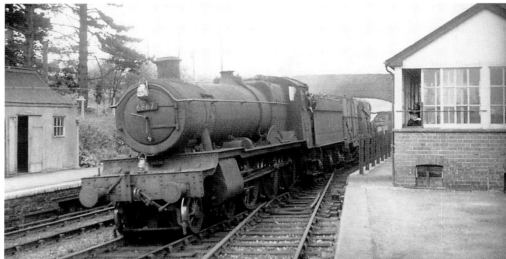

Pontypool Road 'Grange' No.6867 *Peterston Grange* drifting along the gently falling gradient through Nantyderry station with a southbound class 'H' freight on Saturday, 17th May 1958. At this time, Pontypool Road had six 'Granges' to cover five goods turns, mostly on the North & West. The 'Pagoda' shelter on the Up platform provided basic accommodation at this small station, which was not usually troubled by many passengers by this time.   JOHN BEARDSMORE

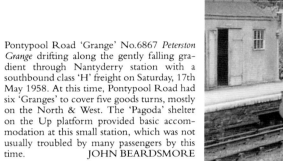

The nameboard for 'Nantyderry for Goytre' features in this view of Pontypool Road's Stanier '8F' 2–8–0 No.48424, seen from the Down platform with an Up class 'H' freight on Saturday, 17th May 1958. The engine was transferred to Chester LMR during the following month, along with several other '8Fs'. One of the Swindon-built batch of late 1943, and allocated to St. Philip's Marsh, No.8424 had been recorded on the North & West as early as August 1946 on a Shrewsbury to Pontypool Road freight, a not uncommon situation at the time as engines wandered away from their home sheds and scheduled duties.   JOHN BEARDSMORE

Recalling scenes of between forty and fifty years earlier, restored 'City' Class No.3440 *City of Truro* was pictured south of Nantyderry with a nine-coach return special working to Cardiff on Tuesday, 27th May 1958. The coaching stock seems to have been a variety of largely ex-LMS vehicles.   R.O. TUCK

Another view of Nantyderry's southern approaches, again at track level, with St. Philips Marsh 'Hall' No.4980 *Wrottesley Hall* piloting Shrewsbury 'County' No. 1016 *County of Hants* on the 8.0 a.m. Plymouth to Liverpool on Saturday, 16th March 1957. At this time of the year, the Saturday trains differed little in composition to their weekday equivalents, with ten vehicles being the usual load without strengthening. R.O. Tuck is seen on the left bank.   JOHN HODGE

LITTLE MILL JUNCTION ₃

Little Mill station (29m 29ch) came into being in January 1854 upon the opening of the main line, and became a junction in June 1856 with the arrival of the Coleford, Monmouth, Usk & Pontypool Railway, but with no facilities for the branch trains. The station, with its two main platforms, closed in October 1861.

A drawing for 1880 shows a small yard to the east of the branch line, with its two short loop sidings associated with the brick traffic from the nearby Little Mill Brick Co. A single dead-end mileage siding was located on the west side of the branch, with the stop block at its north-eastern end. The signal box was located on the Up side, alongside the junction.

In May 1883, a new platform was opened at Little Mill for branch traffic only, this being effectively a sideways-extension of the still-surviving Down Main platform.

In the era of the Jellicoe Specials, the yard was much used as an overspill to Pontypool Road for returning empties.

The small yard alongside the branch line was remodelled around 1922 to cater for overspill coal traffic from Pontypool Road yard, with four long sidings now provided. The signal box was moved closer to the station site around the same time.

In the early 1920s, the Down Main platform (officially unused, but still in situ) was 280ft in length, as was the adjacent Branch platform. There was a single mileage siding of 17-wagon capacity beyond the branch platform, alongside the running line, with a cart weighbridge alongside. The four

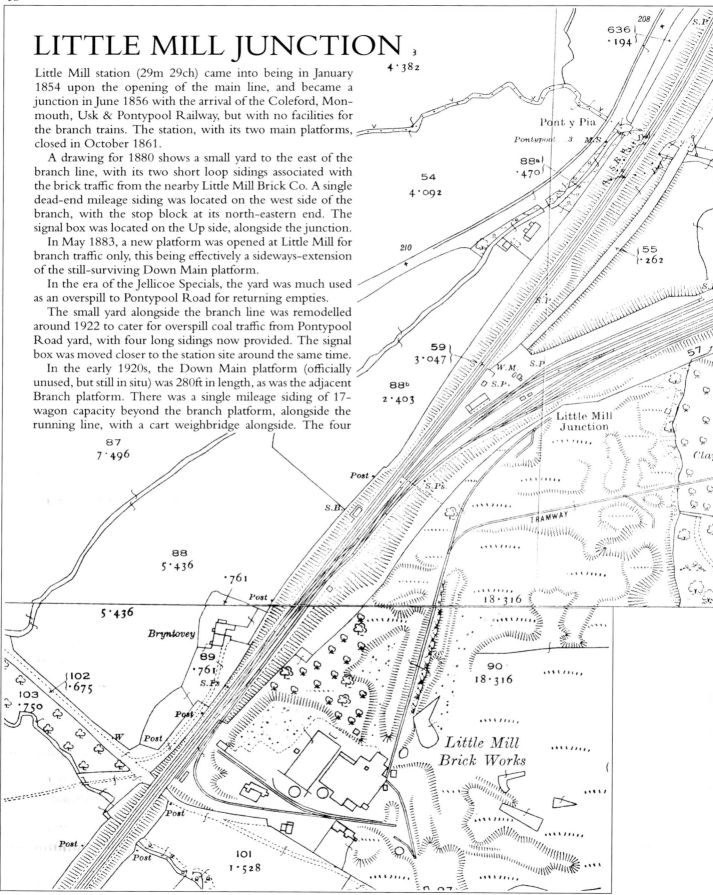

Taken from 25-inch Ordnance Survey for 1920. Crown Copyright reserved.

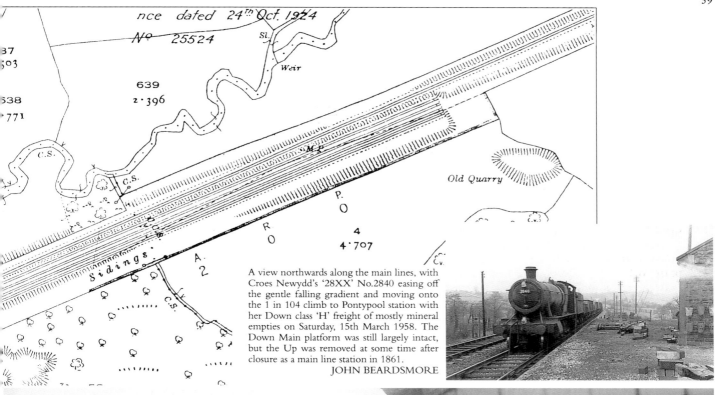

nce dated 24ᵗʰ Oct. 1924
№ 25524

637
503

639
2·396

638
771

Weir
St.

C.S.

C.S.

M.P.

P.
O

R
O

4
4·707

Old Quarry

C.S.

Sidings.

A
2

C.S.

E.

A view northwards along the main lines, with Croes Newydd's '28XX' No.2840 easing off the gentle falling gradient and moving onto the 1 in 104 climb to Pontypool station with her Down class 'H' freight of mostly mineral empties on Saturday, 15th March 1958. The Down Main platform was still largely intact, but the Up was removed at some time after closure as a main line station in 1861.

JOHN BEARDSMORE

Little Mill, facing south from the station platform on 28th July 1963, many years after the withdrawal of branch passenger services to Chepstow, although workmen's trains continued to run to Glascoed until 1961. Branch freight services still operated through the station to Usk at this time. The throat of the yard is seen in the centre, with the water tank to supply the many pilots and train engines that had utilised Little Mill in the past.

P.J. GARLAND

Little Mill station from the Monmouth branch, in a view looking south towards the North & West line on Monday, 11th April 1955. This was probably taken from outside the left-hand side window of the autotrailer's cab as it approached the platform with the 11.48 a.m. service from Monmouth, one of four remaining trains of the eleven recently operating in each direction.

R.M. CASSERLEY

Diesel railcar W30 on the return from Monmouth to Pontypool Road c.1950, calling at Little Mill Junction station. At this time, the car carried out four return trips daily from Pontypool Road to Monmouth (Troy or May Hill), where it met with a Newport diesel on the Chepstow run, and an auto on the Ross services.

STEPHENSON LOCOMOTIVE SCC.

storage sidings in the marshalling yard opposite accommodated 68, 85, 80 and 78 wagons respectively (as from the branch line).

Four more sidings were provided on the south-eastern side of the storage yard around 1937, and the signal box was extended. The final yard layout had seven long and one short sidings. Shunting work at the station was handled by two engines, each working for 7 hours.

The station was closed upon the withdrawal of the Monmouth line services in May 1955, although workmen's services to Glascoed Factory continued until August 1961. Little Mill sidings lasted in traffic until 1964, being much used in later years to store condemned and surplus wagons. Freight services to Usk survived until 1965.

There were also two private sidings at Little Mill, one on the Down side at the south end of the complex leased to the Little Mill Brick Company (c.1860-1966), the other on the up side south of the junction leased to British Nylon Spinners (1947–68).

In 1979, the signal box was converted to a panel box covering the area to Llantarnam Jct.

A view of the junction itself at Little Mill, taken from the branch platform with a 'County' working the northbound 12-coach service 'M12' in this c.1963 photograph. The convergence of the branch and Down Main platforms is seen, with the nameboard most likely only showing its lettering on the near side. DAVID LAWRENCE/ HUGH DAVIES COLLECTION

Little Mill Junction and signal box, looking south on 17th April 1965. The old brickworks siding originally diverged sharply to the left from the spur ahead, whilst to the right, beyond the Up Main bracket signal, was the British Nylon Spinners' siding. The extended box frame contained 55 spaces, eight of which were empty. On the left, the Down bracket signal illustrates examples of siding, stop and backing signals controlling movements to the Spur, Down Main and Up Main Backing from the branch. R.H. MARROWS

Passing the Down Distant signal for Pontypool Road, near Ty-mawr, the shed's 'ROD' No.3038 rounding a curve with a short Class 'H' southbound freight in the early afternoon of Saturday, 28th July 1951. RODs were much used on the North & West during the early 1950s, with seven based at Pontypool Road for its five turns, and others occasionally seen with through freights on the line from St. Philip's Marsh, Canton and Oxley. By this time, they were probably a more common a sight along the N&W than over most other main line sections.
R.O. TUCK

PONTYPOOL ROAD STATION

The north end of Pontypool Road station on Thursday, 26th March 1959, looking north from the platform end, with the North box on the right-hand (Down) side. This southbound Class 'H' freight, headed by Pontypool Road '43XX' 2–6–0 No.5321, had crossed from the Down Main to the Down Goods line running along the west side of the station. The train appears to have had a load of empties on the front, suggesting it may well have been a local service from Hereford which had cleared empties from various yards en route and would terminate in Pontypool Road yard. The engine had been taken out of storage a week earlier, and was in her final six months' spell of duty prior to being condemned in the September.   S RICKARD/J & J COLLECTION

The passenger station at Pontypool Road as we remember it from much of the 20th century, was opened on St. David's Day, 1st March 1909, to replace the previous station which had by that time become inadequate for the volume of traffic handled.

The old Pontypool Road station was located immediately to the south of the overbridge carrying the road from Abergavenny and Pontypool to Newport, in the area opposite the later Pontypool Road South Signal Box. It consisted of Up and Down platforms, the Up being an island platform, with the Vale of Neath and Taff Vale Extension service using the west face. The Down platform, which abutted the considerable main station building, had a bay at its south end; according to a drawing of 1886, this Down bay was not accessible to the Taff Vale Extension line, although it could serve both the connection to the MR&CC Eastern Valleys line, and the PC&N route for Newport.

There was a signal box at each end of the station, named North Nos. 1 and 2, and whilst No. 2 was definitely on the Up side to the north of the overbridge, the exact location of No. 1 (at the south end) is unclear.

Modifications probably took place on the station some fifteen years after its opening, as approval was given to widening, lengthening and covering the Up platform in 1869, whilst a similar agreement confirmed the planned extension of the Down platform in 1875. The station was thus in a better form to accommodate the longer trains envisaged over the new PC&N route.

The new station of 1909, located to the north of the roadbridge, was very different in design to the first. A wide cutting/embankment site was constructed to accommodate the single, large island platform and associated trackwork. The main station building was alongside the embankment on its eastern (Down) side, with its ground floor some feet below rail level, served by an approach road from the nearby main Newport road (The High Way).

This main building was a two-storey structure, with a subway at its south end – at road level – connecting to the platform. Beyond the subway on the ground floor of the main building was the booking hall, booking office, and various staff rooms. The first floor – some 6ft above rail level – contained the superintendent's and other offices.

The subway was 17ft wide, with the 9ft width for passengers segregated from the 8ft for luggage and parcel movements by a railing. It connected to the platform by steps towards its south end.

With a total length of 1,200ft, the platform was of symmetrical construction, able to take the longest N&W services. It contained near identical, single-line bays at each end, the north end bay for the Monmouth services, and the south end bay for the Vale of Neath/Taff Vale Extension (now becoming known throughout as the VoN) route.

The buildings were of considerable architectural elegance, built in red brick, set with blue brick facings, and relieved with Victoria Stone dressings. The largest of these were supported by brick piers and arches set on natural, solid ground, independently arranged to accommodate the differing height of the platform throughout its length. The main building contained waiting and refreshment rooms, with a separate building for the stationmaster, telegraph and parcels offices, and staff accommodation. The upper floor of a two-storey section contained bedrooms and sitting rooms for attendants.

Up and Down Main lines ran alongside the two outer platform faces, connected by scissors crossings half way along the platform length to the adjacent Relief lines. The Up and Down Goods Lines ran on the far west of the station, allowing a clear run for Down trains from leaving the main line at the North box to obtain access to the yard or the Vale of Neath line at South box. Through Down main-line freights not calling at Pontypool Road could also use the Down Main or Relief lines on the east side of the station.

There were three carriage sidings on the east (Down) side, to the north of the main station building, used for holding Vale of Neath, Glascoed Workmen and spare stock for specials (e.g. football or Barry Island). Another, lengthy carriage siding was provided on the Up side, between the Up Relief and Down Goods running lines.

Whilst the roads around the station were primarily concerned with passenger movements, marshalling and stock storage, and through goods running, one Up goods siding was provided off the Up Goods to the north of the road overbridge.

Two main signal boxes controlled movements through the station. Station South box was on the Up side to the south of the road bridge, and Station North box on the Down side beyond the immediate station connections, although to the south of the goods lines junction (North Junction). In the very centre of the station, level with the two scissors crossovers, was the Station Central box, located on the platform; this was only in operation during the hours of normal passenger operations, and before the Great War was closed between 9.10 p.m. and 7.0 a.m. on weekdays, and all day Sundays. It was reduced to a ground frame in 1957.

The station diagrams of the early 1920s give usable main platform lengths of 1,130ft (i.e. without ramps), the North bay of 300ft and the South Bay of 290ft. The three Down side carriage sidings were recorded as 480, 418 and 275ft respectively (as from the Down Relief), and whilst no figure is notated, the Up carriage siding was probably around 1,000ft. The Up goods siding held 72 wagons.

Staff at Pontypool Road station in 1929 amounted to 85, with a Station & Yard Master in control:

Station

Assistant Stationmaster	1
Stationmaster's Clerk	1
Booking Clerks	2
Telegraph Clerks	10
Station Inspectors	3
Ticket Collectors	7
Train Ticket Collector	1
Parcels Porters	2
Porters	8
Telegraph Messengers	3
Waiting Room Attendant	1
Office Messenger	1
Passenger Shunters	7

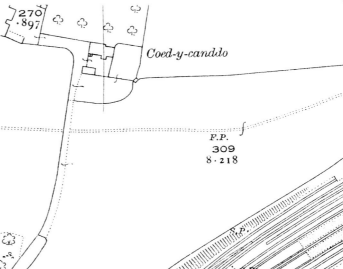

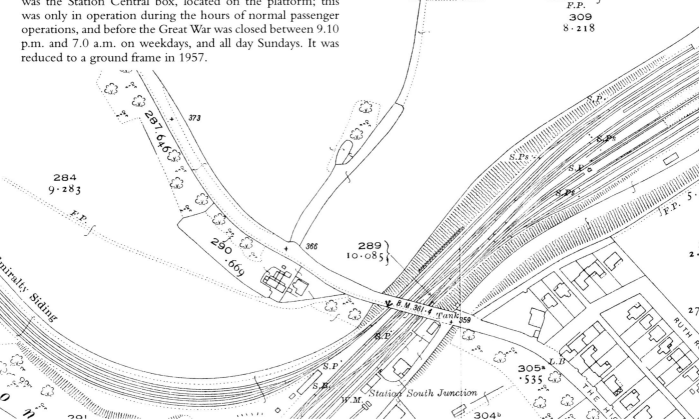

Signalmen:

East	3
West	3
Centre Platform	3
North	3
South	5
Signal Lampman	1
Passenger Guards	17
Porter Guards	2

The next few years saw a reduction in staff, with numbers of telegraph clerks, porters, messengers, passenger shunters and guards removed from the permanent establishment. By

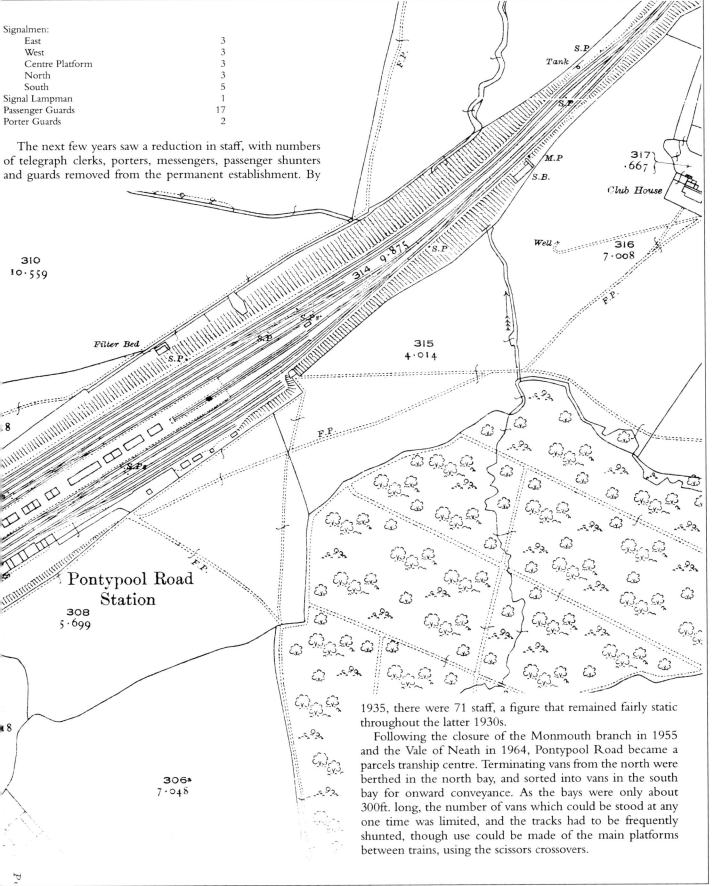

1935, there were 71 staff, a figure that remained fairly static throughout the latter 1930s.

Following the closure of the Monmouth branch in 1955 and the Vale of Neath in 1964, Pontypool Road became a parcels tranship centre. Terminating vans from the north were berthed in the north bay, and sorted into vans in the south bay for onward conveyance. As the bays were only about 300ft. long, the number of vans which could be stood at any one time was limited, and the tracks had to be frequently shunted, though use could be made of the main platforms between trains, using the scissors crossovers.

Pontypool Road's '28XX' No.3824 easing a train of coal empties southwards on the Goods Loop at Pontypool Road on Saturday, 12th October 1957. Running under class 'F' head-lamps, this train was the slowest example of express freight, with no vehicles connected by vacuum pipe to the engine, but able to travel at a speed only slightly less than the 'E' vacuum services; its allowance was 24 minutes from Abergavenny (Monmouth Road) – instead of the 23 minutes of the latter – an average speed of 23½ mph. By this time, steel mineral wagons were more common, and were in the majority at the head of the train.

DAVID JOHNSON COLLECTION

Running past the three-post bracket signal with aspects for the Bay, Down Platform and Down Relief lines, Canton 'Hall' No.6932 *Burwarton Hall* is seen with the 13-coach 11.45 a.m. Manchester to Plymouth into Pontypool Road on Thursday, 26th March 1959, prob-ably substituting for a 'Britannia'. The engine was carrying the winter 1958/9 headcode No.932, which at the time identified the 8.55 a.m. Cardiff to Manchester, its northbound working that morning; it would continue through to Bristol with the Plymouth train, work the 7.15 p.m. (12.0 noon Penzance) back to Pontypool Road and the 12.4 a.m. thence (7.2 p.m. Liverpool) to Cardiff.

S. RICKARD/J & J COLLECTION

Taking water at the column alongside the Up Relief line, Shrewsbury Stanier '8F' No.48470 is seen at the head of a Class 6 ('E') freight on Saturday, 14th September 1963. Running with a vacuum head of three empty opens (etc.), this permitted trains to run at a higher head-code than was common at the time. The 'E' freights were traditionally the preserve of larger-wheeled, mixed traffic locomotives capable of a sustained running of 35 mph (maximum), although the '8Fs' were certainly capable of such speeds.   F.K. DAVIES/
GW TRUST

Ex-LMS '8F' No.48330 leaving the station area on the Up Goods line with a class 'H' freight, and about to join the main line at North Junction. This engine spent some time at Swansea (Paxton St.) during the mid-1950s, working over the former L&NW Central Wales line to Craven Arms and Shrewsbury, but moved to Llanelly shed in September 1959. Its load was primarily (and possibly entirely) made up of steel mineral wagons.
R. H. MARROWS

Looking northwards from the north end of the station with No.44858 easing across onto the Down Main (former Down Relief) with the 9.30 a.m. Manchester to Cardiff and Swansea on Saturday, 14th December 1963. The engine seems to have had a smokebox plate '17B', which had been Burton, and was listed as being from that shed (but as '16F'). The North Bay line is seen to the left, and Down Platform to the right of the photographer.   R.H. MARROWS

Running into the Down Platform, Pontypool Road 'Hall' No.6903 *Belmont Hall* is seen at the head of the 11.45 a.m. Manchester to Plymouth on Saturday, 11th July 1959 as it was approaching the two Down bracket signals; these controlled the movements along and between the Down Platform and Down Relief lines, the latter over the central scissors crossing, with the single, slightly lower arm in each case denoting the slower speed over the crossing. The connection from the Down Platform to the Down Relief line looks little used. The engine was carrying the train number '944' of its previous duty, the 8.15 a.m. Bristol to Crewe, which it traditionally worked northwards from Pontypool Road on summer Saturdays.

H.C. CASSERLEY

Following the closure of the Vale of Neath line in 1964, Pontypool Road became a parcels concentration point, where trains from the North were terminated in the north end (former Monmouth) bay, and new trains started for Cardiff (etc.) in the south bay (former Vale of Neath). This view looks southwards along the Down platform with the north bay on the right, and vans awaiting attention, or empty, on the left, in the old carriage sidings.   LENS OF SUTTON

The Monmouth line service departed from the north bay, and is seen here on Friday, 19th May 1950 worked by Pontypool Road 0–4–2T No. 1422. At this time, only one auto trip was scheduled daily over the branch from Pontypool Road – the 8.33 a.m. to Usk and back – on which a single trailer usually sufficed. The main service to Monmouth, providing four return trips, was worked nominally by a diesel, although the auto was doubtless substituted from time to time.
                                                                                      F.K. DAVIES/GW TRUST

At about 3 p.m., the Longsight engine for the 3.19 p.m. departure to Manchester (the 7.30 a.m. Penzance) would approach the station and stand at the signal on the Up Relief line, waiting to change engines with the Western Region loco that had worked the train from Bristol. In this scene, on Saturday, 9th May 1959, Longsight 'Jubilee' No. 45595 *Southern Rhodesia* was waiting to take over from Bath Road 'County', No. 1009 *County of Carmarthen*, whose fireman is seen jumping down to uncouple.   JOHN HODGE

Good photographic opportunities were provided while the LMR engine was waiting at the Up Relief line signal for its train, as seen here with 'Jubilee' No.45587 *Baroda* on Wednesday, 13th May 1959. A number of fittings (batteries?) had been placed along the footplate for its run from the shed, probably for loading into a van of the Manchester train for onwards movement – it was not unusual to see a light engine used for carrying items over short distances, particularly if it saved a special journey by other means.   JOHN HODGE

The Up platform, looking southwards along its length c.1964. The pannier tank to the right was shunting vans in the two Carriage Sidings, which, with the closure of local services, were probably not much required for storing passenger–carrying stock any more. The platform trolleys, however, were probably more in use than in previous times with the station's enhanced parcels role.   LENS OF SUTTON

It was indeed a treat to see unrebuilt 'Patriots' as far south as Pontypool Road, and here, on Saturday, 14th June 1958, Longsight's No.45505 *The Royal Army Ordnance Corps* was awaiting the arrival of the 7.30 a.m. Penzance, complete with Fowler tender and coal rail.
JOHN HODGE

Ready for departure, No.45505 blowing off at the head of the 7.30 a.m. Penzance, which she would work through to Manchester. In terms of simple tractive effort, the unrebuilt 'Patriot' was similar to a 'Hall', although in its loading, the '6P' was shown between a 'King' and 'Castle'/'County', capable of taking 435 tons between Pontypool Road and Hereford unassisted.   JOHN HODGE

Shorter trains were dealt with centrally on the Up platform as here with the 11.50 a.m. Swansea to Manchester on Saturday, 15th February 1958. Canton's 'Britannia' No.70025 *Western Star* was working through from Cardiff to Shrewsbury, returning to Cardiff with the 3 p.m. Liverpool (5.28 p.m. ex-Shrewsbury). The 11.50 a.m. Swansea train comprised a regular WR five-coach set, with an additional Second on Fridays and Saturdays, and a daily LMR Brake van from Cardiff to Stockport at the rear. As with all Manchester-bound services, the load was not to exceed 9 vehicles for that city.
JOHN HODGE

Shunting empty vans on the Up Relief service, possibly in connection with a Vale of Neath service, locally based '41XX' No.4138 is pictured on Saturday, 31st July 1954. In addition to odd appearances on the through Manchester to Swansea service between Pontypool Road and Cardiff, these engines would work Vale of Neath services and weekend and Bank Holiday 8- or 10-coach excursions from Pontypool Road and Blaenavon to Barry Island, as well as football excursions and other specials from the area. The coaches standing behind the engine were on the nearer of a pair of Carriage Sidings, beyond which were the two Goods lines.
F.K. DAVIES/GW TRUST

A view of the Up Platform (Main) line at the north end of the station from the tender of Canton 'Hall' No.4953 *Pitchford Hall* around mid-day on Friday, 28th September 1951. Two northbound freights were awaiting the road on the Up Goods line to the left; these Goods lines were worked by Permissive Block, which allowed more than one goods, empty stock train or engine to be in the section at the same time. The Station North signal box is seen in the distant centre, and the north bay on the right, with the water crane serving the Down platform and bay lines on the platform between the two.   S.C.L. PHILLIPS/
D.K. JONES COLLECTION

In the last months of steam, No.6658 is seen marshalling some parcels stock in the carriage sidings on the Up side of the station, on 5th April 1965; with the closure of the Monmouth and Vale of Neath lines, and the introduction of DMUs on the remaining local services, the familiar rakes of passenger stock in these sidings had given way to parcels vehicles. No.6658 was a latecomer to Pontypool Road shed, arriving in December 1964 from Rhymney, and she was withdrawn shortly after this photograph was taken.
B.W.L. BROOKSBANK/
INITIAL PHOTOGRAPHICS

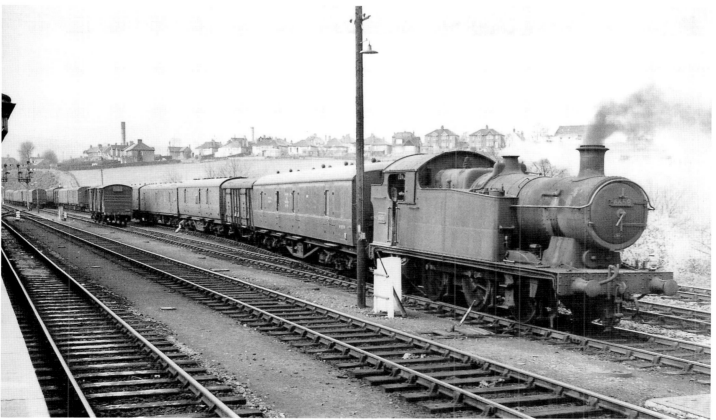

Bath Road 'Modified Hall' No. 7901 *Dodington Hall* is seen leaving the station with the 9.10 a.m. Manchester (London Road) to Swansea train (No. 745) on Thursday, 26th March 1959. Replacing the LMR engine at Pontypool Road, this turn had sometimes been a Pontypool Road '41XX' to Cardiff, but was now (nominally) a Pontypool 'Hall' turn; the engine returned with the through 4.40 p.m. Cardiff to Hereford service, and the 6.42 p.m. Crewe Parcels thence back to Bristol that night. On Thursdays in the winter programme, the 9.10 Manchester was scheduled for a 5-coach rake for Swansea, an LMR Brake Van for Cardiff, and a Brake Compo from Birkenhead to Cardiff at the rear, a formation that had obviously been strengthened on this occasion.
S. RICKARD/J & J COLLECTION

Pontypool Road station, seen from the descending approach road, c. 1962. This affords a good view of the Down side signals, the water cranes and other fittings so typical of this period. The 1,130ft length of the station is also clear, this being sufficient to hold a couple of nine-coach trains if necessary. Although it cannot be seen, Station Middle signal box was located in the centre of the platform about halfway down its length, adjacent to the scissor crossover roads to each side of the island platform. It remained open – if latterly in little use – until 1967.
LENS OF SUTTON

The top of the station approach, where it joins the main A4042 Newport (right) to Pontypool (left) road, seen on 13th July 1958. Notices advertising excursion or cheap day tickets adorned the hoarding, with Barry Island (5s 3d), Penarth (4s 6d) and Porthcawl (7s 6d) featuring. The 'inverted triangle in a circle' sign behind the hoarding probably displayed 'Halt at Major Road Ahead'.

H.C. CASSERLEY

The forecourt side of the main booking and parcels office building, seen from the bottom of the station approach on 1st September 1953. The canopy reached over the main entrance, beyond which was the subway to the island platform. The building also housed the old Pontypool Road Traffic Divisional Superintendent's (South Hereford, Pontypool Road & Neath VoN and branches, up to the Grouping) and General offices. The embankment beyond the building was alongside the Down carriage sidings, which illustrates the track level at this point.

LENS OF SUTTON

A view across the south end of Pontypool Road station, looking east, in early Nationalisation days, showing '43XX' No.7300 awaiting the road with a down freight. '41XX' No.4134 was waiting in the south end bay with a Vale of Neath service, the engine in hybrid form with newly-painted 'British Railways' lettering but still with a painted buffer beam number. The remote main station building on the approach road can be seen in the left background, whilst on the platform, the station nameboard advised passengers to 'Change for Aberdare, Merthyr, Usk, Monmouth and Ross.'

J.G. HUBBACK

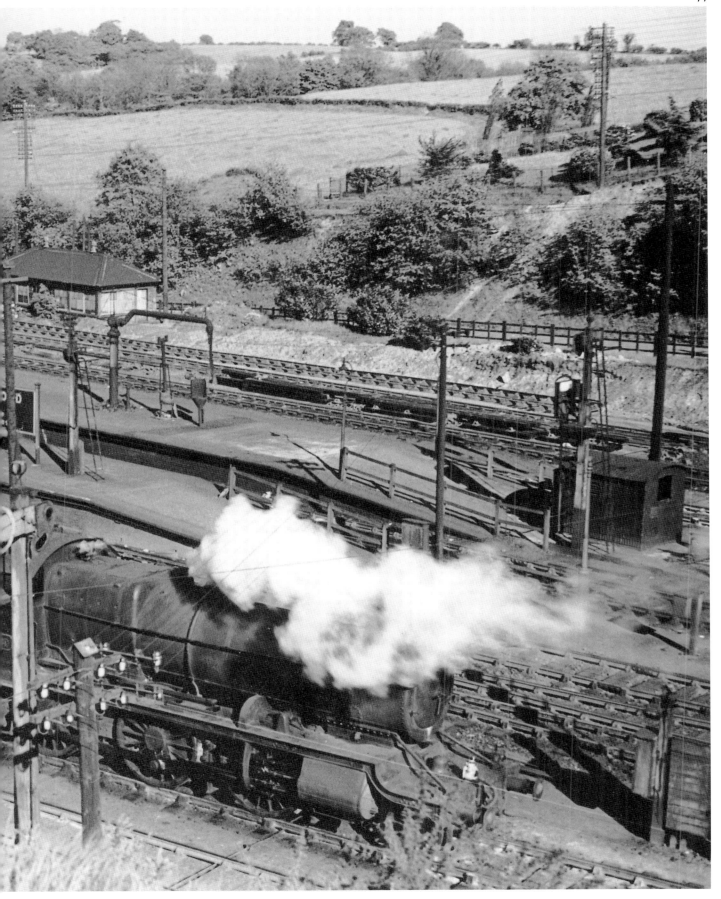

Pontypool Road's importance as a parcels tranship station is clearly evident here, with parcels traffic seen at all points on 27th July 1963. The South Bay was busy with tranship work, with more vans seen against the Down platform and in the carriage sidings beyond. On the right, a parcels train is seen waiting on the Down Relief, possibly with more traffic. Again, the 'Hall' on the engine spur was awaiting her next duty.

P.J. GARLAND

Pontypool Road shed housed a small number of '45XX' 2–6–2 tanks from 1929, when building of the class had been completed. They were used during the 1930s on local passenger duties, and also on the Pontypool Road and Monmouth freights, and in the 1940s they were recorded on various goods workings out as far as Aberbargoed and Aberdare. No.4593 is pictured here standing on the carriage sidings road near the main station building on Thursday, 26th March 1959, with the approach road sloping down behind, and the houses off Ruth Road above.

S. RICKARD/
J & J COLLECTION

Having worked the 7.30 a.m. Penzance to Manchester from Bristol Temple Meads (depart 2.5 p.m.) to Ponty-pool Road, Bath Road 'Castle' No.7003 *Elmley Castle* went on shed for turning and now is seen at the head of the 4.45 p.m. to Cardiff, awaiting access to the Down platform on Thursday, 26th March 1959. The train was formed by the 'classic' GWR/WR 4-coach set (in either corridor or non-corridor stock) of an outer pair of Van Thirds sandwiching a Compo and Third, the third coach of which was probably in choc-olate and cream livery.

S. RICKARD/
J & J COLLECTION

Just after allocation to Cardiff Canton in April 1962, and following a Heavy Intermediate at Swindon, 'Castle' No.5043 *Earl of Mount Edgecumbe* is seen here at the down platform with the 3 p.m. Liverpool to Cardiff. Up to that time, her career had been spent almost exclusively at Old Oak Common (since new in 1936), other than spells at Swindon in 1941/2 and Carmarthen in 1952–56). Owing to the weight of passenger traffic, this service was running divided from the Manchester/Glasgow to Plymouth portion – which was usually attached to the rear – on this Easter Monday, 23rd April 1962. MICHAEL MENSING

About to change engines on the 3.5 p.m. Manchester to Plymouth (with through coaches from Glasgow), Pontypool Road 'Grange' No.6820 *Kingstone Grange* would hand over to another locally based 'Grange' standing on the Down Relief line on Easter Monday, 23rd April 1962. Pontypool Road shed had a couple of express passenger/parcels turns daily, utilising its 'Halls' or 'Granges', but this usage was doubled on Friday nights/Saturdays in peak traffic periods. The end of Pontypool Road's South box can be glimpsed between the canopy support girders, beyond The Highway road bridge.

MICHAEL MENSING

A panoramic view to the south of the station, taken from the Down platform on Monday, 11th April 1955, looking towards Newport. The station approach road is seen to the left, sweeping up to join the road that the bridge in the middle distance carried towards Pontypool; the town centre was a little over a mile away, to the right. The 'Grange' in the engine spur was waiting to take over a down passenger service. The Station South box can just be seen through the 'Grange's' exhaust, beyond the arch; South's home signals controlling departure from the platforms and main lines are seen beyond the platform ends and off to the right a rake of empty Open wagons out of Pilkingtons feature.   H.C. CASSERLEY

No.8444 was an Aberdare engine, and is seen here with a Vale of Neath service on Friday, 18th April 1958. With the sun in the west, this was probably the 5.0 p.m. train to Aberdare (High Level), scheduled to take 63 minutes for the 22¾-mile journey.   COLLECTION D.K. JONES

On Thursday, 6th June 1963, Shrewsbury's 'Jubilee' No.45660 *Rooke* is seen taking water while it was waiting at the Down platform with the 3.35 p.m. Liverpool (Lime St.) to Cardiff. The five-minute call at Pontypool Road was sufficient to top up after the 46-minute run from Hereford, and would easily take the engine to Cardiff; an intermediate stop at Newport was not intended as a water stop, so this was the best occasion to fill up the tender.   R.H. MARROWS

Waiting the road at the south end of the station, Pontypool Road '56XX' 0–6–2T No. 6687 is pictured on the Down Relief line faced by another pair of impressive bracket signals in 1953. At this time, the shed was provided with nine '56XXs' for seven turns, primarily goods work. In the distance, a bus can be seen crossing the bridge that carried the roadway to Pontypool ('The High Way' in earlier times), with the station approach road descending along the face of the nearby cutting to the left of the engine, and the houses on Ruth Road (in Pontypool Road) above.

R.W. HINTON

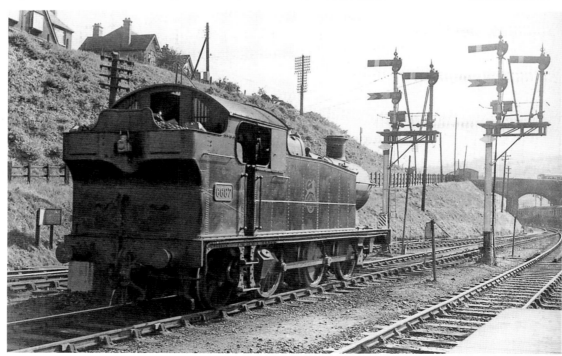

83

The empty south end bay seen on 11th April 1955 from the end of the Down platform ramp, awaiting the arrival of the next Vale of Neath service, its approach controlled from Pontypool Road Station South box. Empty stock – corridor and non-corridor – was as usual standing in the carriage sidings on the left, located between the Up Relief and Down Goods running lines. The stop block on the right was for the engine spur, conveniently situated for engine changing of Down trains.
H.C. CASSERLEY

A scene at the south end of the station on Tuesday, 16th April 1963 with Pontypool Road's '57XX' No. 9650 arriving with the three-coach 11.7 a.m. Neath (due 1.14 p.m.), and entering the South bay. On the left, St. Philip's Marsh 'County' No. 1020 *County of Monmouth* was waiting with the 9.5 a.m. Liverpool to Plymouth, which was due to leave at 1.6 p.m., and may have been running late. The water crane located centrally on the left arm of the platform was to equally serve the Down Main and Bay lines.
R.H. MARROWS

Coleham 'Castle' No.5038 *Morlais Castle* is pictured at the south end of the Down platform awaiting the road with (probably) a Bristol-bound train in January 1962. The engine was nearing the end of its 4-year association with Shrewsbury shed, and in three months time would be transferred to Oxford and Reading sheds for generally rather less demanding duties. She was withdrawn from traffic at Reading in September 1963.

PAUL CHANCELLOR COLLECTION

Banbury '28XX' ('2884' series) class No.3856 on the Up Goods line at the south end of the station with empty iron ore hoppers on Thursday, 26th March 1959, seen from the approach road. There were four or five iron ore services daily at this time running from Banbury (Oxfordshire Iron Ore Co.) to Cardiff (GKI&S) and Margam (SCOW) via Stratford-upon-Avon and Gloucester, returning the empties from either Margam or Cardiff mainly by the same route, although a couple ran via Hereford, Worcester, Honeybourne and Stratford; the train pictured here was possibly the 11.40 a.m. Cardiff, which took the latter (N&W) route home.

S. RICKARD/J & J COLLECTION

A variety of power was used on the Vale of Neath passenger services in the 1950s and early 60s, with '41XXs', '56XXs', '84XXs' and '57XXs' common, as well as '43XXs' and even the odd 4–6–0. Seen from the station approach road, Pontypool Road 'Mogul' No.7325 is pictured pulling away from the Down platform with the four-coach 2.25 p.m. to Neath on Thursday, 26th March 1959, the route signal for which can be seen above the last coach. The empty mineral wagons on the left are probably out of Pilkington's private siding.

S. RICKARD/D.K. JONES COLLECTION

Another panoramic view of the south end of Pontypool Road station, seen from the road bridge on 27th June 1963, with a Stanier '8F' waiting the road on the Down Goods line and a grimy 'Hall' in the engine spur waiting to take over a southbound working. The whole complex of running lines, sidings and crossovers is clearly visible in this photograph, including empty wagons out of Pilkingtons standing on the extreme left. The increasing use as a parcels tranship centre is evidenced by the vans in the South Bay, and by those standing in the two carriage sidings to the left of the station.

P.J. GARLAND

About to move off the train after working in from Manchester, Longsight 'Jubilee' No.45644 *Howe* is seen at the down platform with the 9.15 a.m. Manchester to Swansea (W210) on Thursday, 26th March 1959. The LMR train number did not coincide with the winter 1958/9 Western Region number – 745 – which was probably conveyed, onwards by the WR engine. In the following summer, the LMR code would be '1612' to Pontypool Road, and the WR '717' on to Swansea.

RICKARD/J & J COLLECTION

Fortunately, water falling from the sky to replenish supplies is plentiful in South Wales. Here No. 8445 of Aberdare was having her tanks refilled in the south end bay on Saturday, 23rd August 1958. Recently back from overhaul at Wolverhampton, the engine would next work a Vale of Neath service back to Aberdare. On the board behind the engine, only Aberdare and Merthyr now remained as onward destinations connecting at Pontypool Road.

F.K. DAVIES/GW TRUST

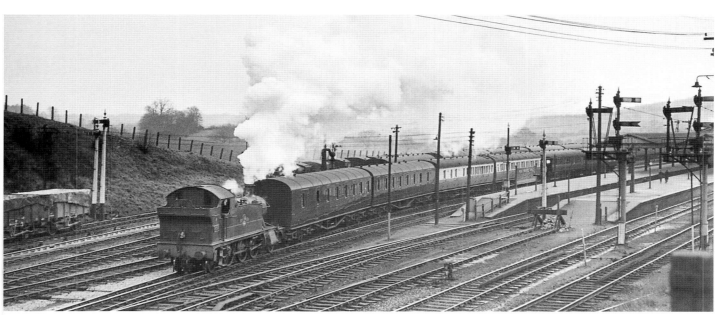

The Pontypool Road-based '45XXs' were used on a variety of duties including banking, and here No. 4593 was shunting passenger stock on the Up Relief line at the station on 26th March 1959. The stock appears to have been a 'B-set' and a four-coach rake of corridor coaches. S. RICKARD/J & J COLLECTION

Pontypool Road, Aberdare and Neath all provided power for Vale of Neath services, and here Aberdare's '56XX' No. 6661, presented in typical Aberdare style, is seen pulling out of the bay platform with the 11.0 a.m. to Neath on Easter Monday, 23rd April 1962. Being classed as a main line, Vale of Neath services were provided with corridor stock, doubtless more comfortable for passengers on this 1hr 57min, 41¾-mile journey. This 4-coach train had previously worked in to Pontypool Road as the 7.40 a.m. from Neath. MICHAEL MENSING

The '57XX' pannier tanks were a most versatile class, with sufficient power and route availability to fulfill a host of lesser traffic requirements. Pontypool Road had around 27 examples for its light freight and shunting turns in the late 1950s, and the shed's No. 4642 is seen here around 11.0 a.m. with the 9.25 a.m. Usk and Glascoed class 'K' freight en route to the yard on Thursday, 26th March 1959. The train was formed with a variety of Open (mostly sheeted) and Covered goods wagons, with a few containers, within its two-dozen (or so) length.
S. RICKARD/
J & J COLLECTION

On the double-home turn to Newton Abbot, Shrewsbury 'County' No. 1025 *County of Radnor* is pictured pulling away from Pontypool Road with the twelve-coach 9.5 a.m. Liverpool to Plymouth on Saturday, 17th September 1955. The Shrewsbury part of this shared turn with Newton Abbot was worked by both 'Castles' and 'Counties', and it was apparently left to driver choice as to which class of engine would be used on the day. The station platform was shown as 1,130ft in length (1920s), sufficient for 18 modern coaches.
JOHN HODGE

The now preserved 'Modified Hall' No.6998 *Burton Agnes Hall* of Cardiff Canton is seen here leaving Pontypool Road with the 1.44 p.m. Hereford to Cardiff (2.56 p.m. Pontypool Road) stopper on Saturday, 17th September 1955. The train comprised a four-coach corridor set, with a five-coach corridor set attached from Pontypool Road to Cardiff on Saturdays only. By the smoke from the rear of the train, the service may have had a helping hand on the 1 in 119 rising gradient out of the station on its way to calls at Lower Pontnewydd, Newport and Cardiff.

JOHN HODGE

Canton '28XX' No.3 817 accelerating away from Pontypool Road station on the Down Goods line with a class 'H' Saltney or Coton Hill to Cardiff Pengam service on Saturday, 17th September 1955. The '28XX' could take 100 such merchandise wagons from Pontypool Road yard to Cardiff, but during the daytime was generally restricted to less to ease its passage amongst the passenger trains operating in the area.

JOHN HODGE

Canton 'Castle' No.7011 *Banbury Castle* departing from Pontypool Road with a southbound service on Saturday, 3rd September 1960. The hastily-chalked '1M65' on the smokebox door probably indicates its outbound duty, the 12.5 a.m. Cardiff to Liverpool, and its unknown return working is seen here in late afternoon – possibly the 11.42 a.m. Manchester (Victoria) to Cardiff, with a scheduled departure from Pontypool Road at 4.48 p.m. A Down freight was standing on the goods line to the left with a DMU in the down bay.
B.K.B GREEN COLLECTION/
INITIAL PHOTOGRAPHICS

Photographed from the roadbridge, Canton 'King' No.6023 *King Edward II* was pulling the 12.15 p.m. Manchester to Plymouth out of the station, working through from Shrewsbury to Bristol on Saturday, 19th May 1962. Exactly one month later, the engine was withdrawn, but good luck shone on it afterwards as she was first sold to T.W. Ward at Briton Ferry (where she would have been cut up), but was then sold on to Woodhams at Barry, who soon sold her on again to Harvey's of Bristol. Following restoration she now lives again, at Didcot. Also illustrated in the picture are a '57XX' 0–6–0PT with the Vale of Neath train in the South Bay, with a good selection of passenger stock in the two carriage sidings to the west of the station.
R.O. TUCK

This train of empty Opens had, rather unusually, been routed along the Down Platform road, perhaps because it was not due to call at Pontypool Road and was given a clear road through, or possibly due to its point of termination in the nearby yards. The engine, '2884' Class 2–8–0 No.2885, was probably from the Birmingham area, and the train was running as a Class 'J' (Class '9' from June 1960). AUTHOR'S COLLECTION

This picture, taken from the road bridge looking north, gives an uninterrupted view of the southern throat of the station. The various roads feeding into the Down Main (bottom, centre right) required a three-way point to enable the connections to be made before reaching the various other crossings immediately to its south.

SIMON JONES

The view south from the roadbridge on 27th July 1963, showing the main line to Newport curving off to the right, and the Vale of Neath line swinging off to the left, access to the engine shed and freight yard complex in the centre, and the Vale of Neath line swinging off to the right. In the foreground, Pontypool Road Station South box is seen on the extreme right, with its two extended bay windows on the front elevation for monitoring movements. Pontypool Road's modest goods yard features on the left – on the site of the original passenger station – with its lock-up and small loading platform to the extreme left, and two sidings beyond (the far with loading bank/carriage landing off the view, further to the left).

P.J. GARLAND

PONTYPOOL ROAD SOUTH & YARDS

A short, 'H' (post-1950) headcode freight passing under the roadbridge at the south end of Pontypool Road station and past the Station South box, heading for the yard, Newport or perhaps Cardiff, behind Gloucester 2–8–0 No.2823 in March 1952. In addition to a few Opens and Vans at the head, the train was also conveying bogie bolster wagons with their loads apparently sheeted. The loading gauge in Pontypool Road's small, local goods yard features in the foreground, to the right.
G.W. SHARPE COLLECTION

The early association of the NA&HR with the S&H and L&NWR contributed much to the flow of coal traffic from South Wales to destinations such as Birkenhead Docks (for bunkers) and Manchester (for industrial and railway use). Pontypool Road became an instant and natural collection point for such northbound traffic, which could emanate from the Vale of Neath, Taff Vale Extension and Eastern Valley collieries.

From the mid-1860s to the early 1870s, the sidings lay around the Pontypool Road Station South & Coedygric Junctions line, to the south of the Taff Vale Extension, and as far down as Coedygric Jct. with the MR&C Eastern Valleys line. Two main yards appear, with one around half-way between the two junctions mentioned, containing three or four sidings on each side of the running lines; this yard was also connected to the TVE, and probably dealt mostly with interchange traffic to and from that line. The second yard was further south, just to the north of Coedygric Jct., and handled interchange traffic with the Eastern Valley route.

Additional goods traffic came from the main line via Newport after the construction of the Pontypool, Caerleon & Newport in 1874.

With traffic to and from local works, Pontypool Road marshalling yard quickly took on considerable proportions, and a plan of the area for 1885 shows much of the final yard arrangements to have been in position by then. Again, the yard was mostly developed to the north of Coedygric Junction signal box, and from 1865 included a new engine shed to replace the original NA&HR shed just south of Coedygric.

At Coedygric Junction, within the 'v' formed between the Eastern Valleys line and that to Pontypool Road South, were five loop sidings, which in later years became known as the

'Old Yard' and were among the original yard sidings, still dealing with the interchange between the two lines as mentioned above.

On the opposite (east) side was a bank of sidings believed to have been known as the 'Coedygric'. Just to the north, the 'Middle' sidings were to the west, with the 'Birkenhead' group to their north, stretching towards Pontypool Road South Junction. On the east side were the 'South' sidings, with the new engine shed beyond them.

In the years following the opening of the PC&N, the yard was extended further, not only with sidings but also with interlinking goods running lines; included in these were connecting lines between the yard and both the northern (at East Junction) and southern (at Panteg Junction) parts of the new line.

In the yards, incoming trains were received either on a reception road attached to the five Coedygric Sidings, or into the double-ended sidings themselves. These were later expanded with a nest of five more sidings nearer to the PC&N line, named 'New Sidings', and the whole of the Coedygric and New Sidings complex would have been used for shunting wagons from through and terminating trains for transfer to the respective group of sidings for onward movement. The goods running lines from East Jct. at this time passed between Coedygric and New sidings.

To the west of the goods running lines that came off the Taff Vale Extension and ran through the yard to eventually join the main line at Panteg, was a group of eleven stop-blocked 'Middle' Sidings, and given their proximity to the Vale of Neath line they were probably used for traffic to that line.

Approaching Pontypool Road from the Newport direction, Bath Road 'Castle' No.7003 *Elmley Castle* is seen heading the 13-coach 7.30 a.m. Penzance to Manchester service past the local goods yard, to the left of the picture, on Thursday, 26th March 1959. The 'Castle' would hand over to Longsight 'Jubilee' No.45644 *Howe* at the station. The northern edge of the engine shed can just be seen beyond the bend around which the train was passing, to the left of the rear coach. The Vale of Neath line can be seen diverging to the right, at top right.

S. RICKARD/
J & J COLLECTION

Pontypool Road Station South signal box was located on the south side of the road bridge, to the west (Up) side of the running lines, and was by far the largest in the area. Opened in 1910, the box was some 70ft in length, and contained a 163-lever frame. The bricked-up windows to the frame room were probably a wartime measure, whilst the cabin had two bay boxes on the frontage to provide signalmen with a convenient platform to view traffic movements, and to check tail lamps, which might otherwise have been obscured by long runs of lever frames and instrumentation. The box remained in service until long after the steam era.

D.K. JONES

A pilot movement outside the Station South box is captured in these 26th March 1959 views of the southern approaches to the station. In the first picture, one of Pontypool Road's '57XX' panniers, No. 3708, is seen running gently past the box, signalled for the Up Goods running line with a transfer freight. It had probably emerged from Birkenhead Sidings, directly behind its train, and is seen with a shunting truck behind the engine. In the second view, having firstly moved along the Up Goods line clear of the pointwork in front of the box, it was being propelled across the main lines to Northern Sidings, which were around the corner on the Down side of the running lines, opposite the engine shed. The old Admiralty Sidings, now in use by Pilkingtons, can be seen behind the box.

S. RICKARD/J & J COLLECTION

Marshalling of the longest trains for the main line would have taken place in a group of double-ended sidings west of the engine shed, the 'South' Sidings and 'Birkenhead' Sidings. Of these, the former was used for traffic to South and West Wales via the Main Line, and the South and West of England via Severn Tunnel Junction. The 'Birkenhead' Sidings went back to the origins of the yard when large amounts of coal were conveyed to Birkenhead Docks, due to the association between the NA&H and L&NWR. It is very likely that coal for the L&NWR northern engine sheds also went from South Wales via these sidings.

Another set of four sidings with headshunt was provided to the east of the PC&N line, alongside the East box. This was the later 'Northern' sidings site.

The requirement to service the World War I British Fleet at Scapa Flow with South Wales steam coal by rail – because of the risk of sea attack by enemy submarines – caused Pontypool Road to be selected as the collection point for coal emanating from steam coal producing collieries in the Aberdare and Rhondda areas. With the complexity of operation at Pontypool Road Yard at this time, it would have been impossible to guarantee an efficient and regular flow of this vital traffic on which the future of the nation could depend, so the Admiralty, in approving Pontypool Road as the location for the collection of traffic, financed the building of four new sidings just to the west of the Station South signal box, well away from the complexity of yard operations. These sidings, believed to have been opened in 1916, were employed in marshalling Admiralty coal traffic using the N&W route, which, between 26th August 1914 and 30th November 1918, amounted to 11,560 trains conveying 523,793 ten-ton coal wagons. The sidings remained in use throughout that war, but in later years became superfluous and were removed, the area being taken over by Pilkington Glass Works in the 1930s.

The various yards at Pontypool Road were recorded at the Grouping as having the following capacities:

Yard	Sdgs	Capacity
Old	5	146
	H'shunt	5
Transfer Shed & Sdgs	2	74
Coedygric	6	299
New	5	223
Middle	11	226
Birkenhead	7	177
South	10	323
('Northern' site)	4	118
	H'shunt	23

In 1929, the staff in the yards were under the control of the Station & Yard Master:

Yard

General Clerk	1
Yard Inspectors	6
Call Boys	3
Yard Foremen	2
Goods Shunters	46
Signalmen:	
Coedygric	3
South Jct.	3
Middle Jct.	3
Timekeepers	3
Goods Guards	81

Further expansion and remodelling of the yard took place during the mid-1930s. Generally, many sidings were lengthened to facilitate the formation and handling of longer trains. This was contained within a general remodelling of the yard in October 1936 to produce the layout that existed into the 1950s. One of the changes was the combination of the

Coedygric and New sidings, with a central reception road, and the diversion of the East Jct. to Coedygric Jct. running loop to now skirt around their western edge, alongside the goods transfer shed.

With so many sets of sidings forming the overall yard, many individual shunting engines were needed to keep the yard fluid. In his book *On The Footplate* (Bradford Barton, 1976), John Drayton describes his days working at Pontypool Road as a fireman, then driver, starting in the 1930s, and lists the allocation of Pilot engines one day in 1935:

East Banker and Pilot:	4504
Loop or Middle Yard Pilot:	2009
Birkenhead Pilot:	2021
New Sidings Pilot:	2035
Cwmbran (Transfer) Pilot:	2077
Old Yard Pilot:	2140
South Sidings Pilot:	349
Coedygric Pilot:	2080
Panteg (Transfer) Pilot:	2160
Little Mill (Transfer) Pilot:	1730

The Summer 1936 WTT showed the following shunting engine requirements in the Pontypool Road yards:

1.	South Junction Pilot	133½ hrs/week
2.	Old Yard Pilot	139 hrs/week, traffic distribution
3.	East Jct. Pilot	92½ hrs/week, includes banking VoN traffic
4.	Loop Pilot	134 hrs/week
5.	New Sidings Pilot	144 hrs/week
6.	Coedygric Pilot	139 hrs/week. Also trips to other yards & shunts Panteg & Griffithstown
7.	Birkenhead Sidings Pilot	85 hrs/week, banks as required

Work was also carried out by three other engines, including an additional, short duty at Coedygric Sidings, though mostly banking trains leaving the yard.

The Second World War saw another increase in freight traffic to cater for the growth of local industry and the Glascoed Ordnance Factory traffic, and this produced a further increase in the yard facilities. The main creation was a set of nine sidings, stop-blocked to the south, located outside the main yard area on the Down side of the PC&N line, these being termed 'Northern Sidings'. Brought into use during July 1941, they replaced the former four sidings and headshunt arrangement on the site.

Changes in traffic flows, and the NCB decision to make areas self sufficient for coal supply in all but the most demanding cases put an end to much of the South Wales industrial coal traffic to northern destinations as well as domestic flows, other than those for the patent fuels and anthracite not manufactured elsewhere. The last criterion affected this area as Phurnacite smokeless fuel was only manufactured at the Abercwmboi plant, and was distributed throughout the country, much passing from Aberdare to Pontypool Road for onward services. Though Phurnacite traffic for Scotland ran on a through train from Abercwmboi at 7.25 a.m. on Mondays through to Bamfurlong, other Northern traffic was taken to Aberdare and Pontypool Road for staging through Saltney. Anthracite, produced in the western section of the South

Wales coalfield, passed mainly through Margam, from where services ran into England.

A number of circumstances combined to reduce the volume of coal traffic passing through Pontypool Road Yard: colliery closures through exhaustion; a reduction in demand as households moved away from coal to heat homes; development of more block train working from colliery to destination to replace the need for en route marshalling; and more modern techniques of blending coals within washeries, with underground linking to avoid overground transit.

In addition, the general freight side was also diminishing as more and more traffic began to pass by road, with railways forced to reveal their rates which road hauliers could then undercut. Additionally, Cardiff (Pengam), Alexandra Dock Jct. and Rogerstone now had their own through services to Saltney and Coton Hill, rendering the need for similar services from Pontypool Road superfluous.

In the early 1960s, the Hafodyrynys-Margam Steel Works coking coal flow became a figurehead for future development, with the coal conveyed in complete fully-fitted trains of new 21-ton 'Minfits' in 35-wagon lengths, double-headed by two 1750HP diesels, the trains running as the highest category freight, first Class 6, then Class 4 under the later operation, running two round trips per day. With Pontypool Road men working through to Margam and back, this was truly a state-of-the-art operation as far as coal working in South Wales was concerned. By blending its own produce with coal received – eventually by underground linking of the collieries – from Llanhilleth, Blaensychan and Tirpentwys, Hafodyrynys produced a top quality coking coal much acclaimed by NCB and

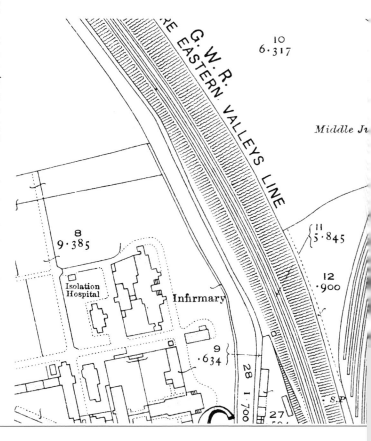

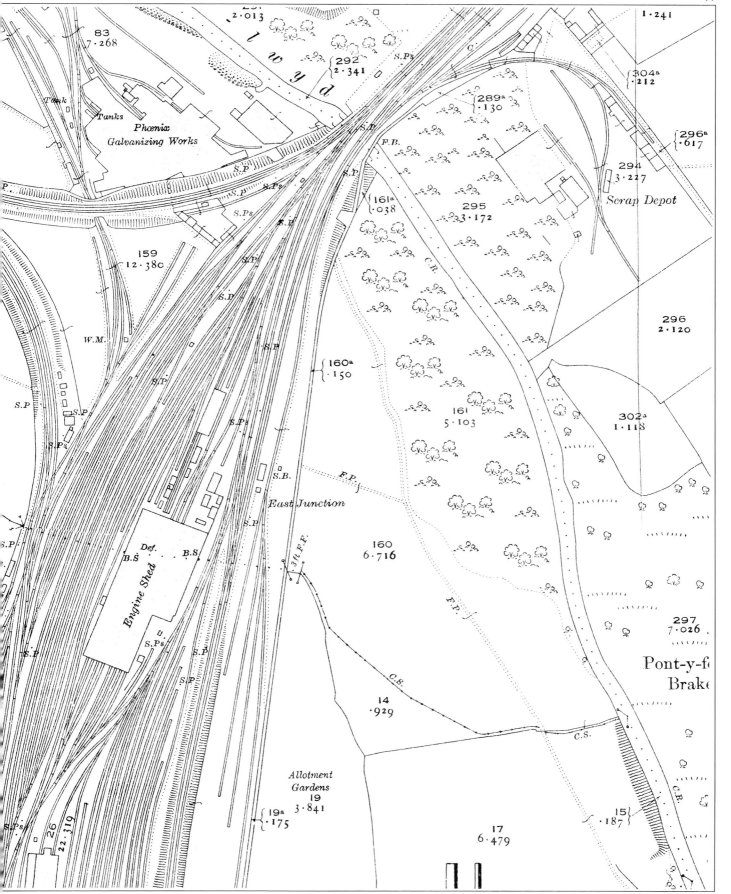

1·241

83
7·268

{ 2·013

l w y d

Tank

Tanks

Phœnix
Galvanizing Works

292
2·341

S.Ps

289ª
·130

304ª
212

S.P.

F.B.

C.

296ª
·617

294
3·227

Scrap Depot

S.P

S.P

S.P

S.Ps

S.P

S.Ps

S.P

161ª
·038

295
3·172

C.R.

296
2·120

159
12·380

S.P

S.P

W.M.

S.P

160ª
·150

161
5·103

302ª
1·118

S.P

S.P

S.Ps

S.Ps

Def.
B.S   B.S

Engine Shed

S.P

S.Ps

S.P

S.P

S.P

26
22·319

S.Ps

S.B.

East Junction

F.P.

314.F.F.

F.P.

160
6·716

C.B.

14
·929

Allotment
Gardens
19
3·841

19ª
·175

C.S.

15
·187

17
6·479

297
7·026

Pont-y-f
Brake

C.R.

East Junction box, looking south-east, as St. Philip's Marsh 'Grange' No.6842 *Nunhold Grange*, was passing along the Up Main with a class 'C' vacuum train in the late 1950s. At this point, Up and Down goods lines (foreground) still ran alongside the Up and Down Mains (the latter being the closer to the signal box) and formed a double junction with them to the right of the box before cutting inwards to round Coedygric and New Siding en route to the Eastern Valleys line at Panteg and Griffithstown.

PAUL CHANCELLOR COLLECTION

Pontypool Road yards on 3rd June 1963, with the engine shed at their centre, looking north towards the station. The photograph was probably taken from the viaduct at the point where it crossed over New Sidings, with the main line immediately to the right, and Northern Sidings beyond on the far right, with East Junction box in the middle distance between them. Beyond East Junction, a set of Goods running lines accompanied the main lines, to their left, as far as TVE Jct., where they joined the Vale of Neath route to pass through the station to the west of the platform. The rake of cattle wagons on the left illustrate that livestock traffic was still evident in South Wales, though a shadow of its former self.

MICHAEL HALE

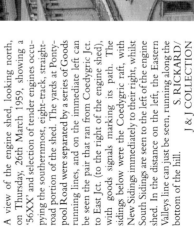

A view of the engine shed, looking north, on Thursday, 26th March 1959, showing a '56XX' and selection of tender engines occupying the southernmost, eight-track, straight-road portion of the shed. The yards at Pontypool Road were separated by a series of Goods running lines, and on the immediate left can be seen the pair that ran from Coedygric Jct. to East Jct. (to the right of the engine shed), with goods signals marking its path. The sidings below were the Coedygric raft, with New Sidings immediately to their right, whilst South Sidings are seen to the left of the engine shed. In the distance on the left, the Eastern Valleys line can just be seen, running along the bottom of the hill.

S. RICKARD/
J & J COLLECTION

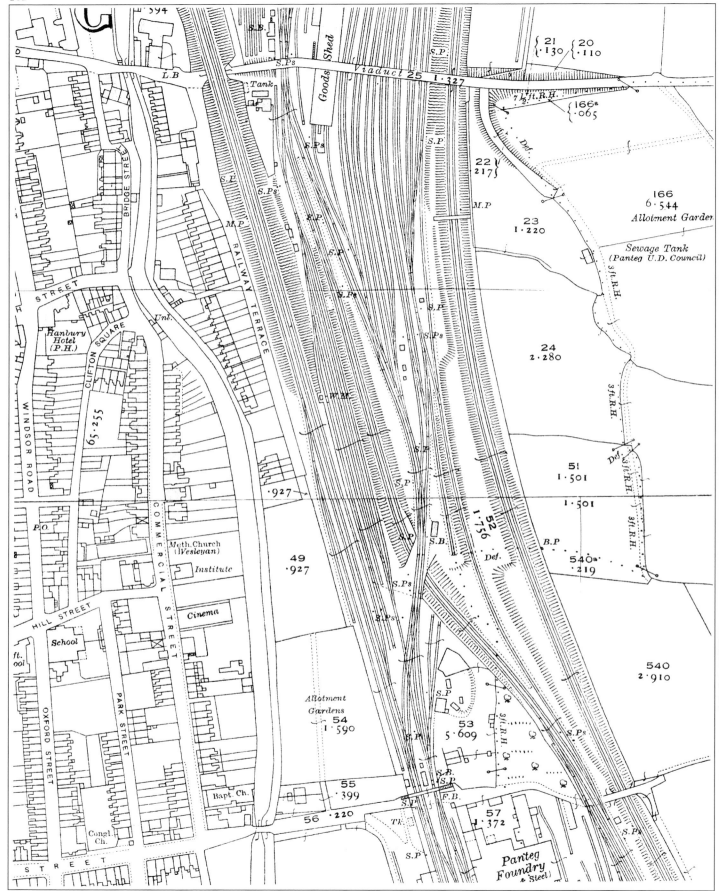

BSC management, which, with a long run to Margam at a good rate, made BR, NCB and BSC management very happy as a pointer to the future.

This principle of fully-fitted trains in 21-ton Minfits (stencilled 'To Work Within South Wales and Monmouthshire Only') was extended into the Western, Rhondda, Rhymney and Bridgend Valleys and considerably improved upon by tighter management control of operations at the end of the 1960s. The mid-1960s saw English Electric Type 3 diesels introduced throughout South Wales for coal working, and when direct colliery to steelworks and power station working was instituted at the end of the decade, the main services to

Margam and Llanwern were operated by Type 4 diesels running as highest category freight services.

Following the closure of the Vale of Neath as a through route in June 1964, the volume of traffic passing through the yard was substantially reduced. A management decision was made in 1965 to close Pontypool Road as a marshalling yard, and deal with the traffic through Alexandra Dock Junction Yard, Newport. This was at a time when there were vast numbers of empty wagons lying around for want of traffic, in addition to the equally large numbers of condemned wagons waiting disposal. The effect of the concentration on AD Jct. was chaotic, and within days the yard was on stop, with all

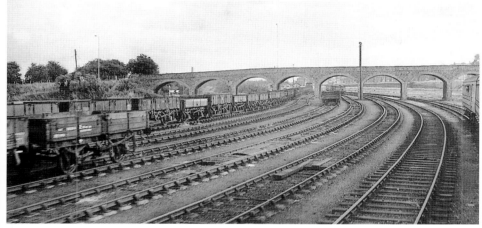

The viaduct that crossed the site connected Griffithstown (Coedygric Road – to the right), with the Newport & Pontypool main road (A4042) at Pontypool Road (New Inn – to the left). It is seen here in 1969, at its eastern end, from a northbound train on the main line, with Northern Sidings to the left. Through the arches behind the train can be seen the former trackbed for the New and Coedygric Sidings, with the ex-Eastern Valleys route at Griffithstown on the far side.
STEPHENSON LOCOMOTIVE SOCIETY

South Junction signal box, seen from the viaduct on Thursday, 26th March 1959, with the Eastern Valleys line at high level climbing at a 1 in 54 gradient in the background. Pontypool Road's No.5750 was shunting on the Goods running line, buffered to a Rogerstone brake van, with Middle Sidings behind. This box, with its single bay platform projection to the front, was at the junction of four 'internal' goods routes: to the left was the junction between the Panteg and Coedygric lines, and just to the right was that between the West Junction (for Aberdare) and North Junctions (for station) routes, each on the Vale of Neath's main line.
S. RICKARD/J & J COLLECTION

sidings full and the yard unable to be worked further. Possibly suffering the effect of too many empty and condemned wagons being moved to AD Jct., it took much organising to get the yard working fluently again, advantage no doubt being taken to move all spare and condemned wagons to surrounding yards, such as Maesglas, Rogerstone, the Cardiff Yards and the huge Docks complex at Newport Mon Bank, and East and West Mendalgief Yards, and no doubt back to Pontypool Road.

It might have been possible that the section of the Vale of Neath line between Crumlin Junction (just east of the viaduct) and Hafodyrynys Colliery would be retained in order to transport coal for washing and blending from Llanhilleth (just south of Aberbeeg and the link line from the Western Valley to Crumlin Junction), in order to avoid the long journey south from Llanhilleth via Rogerstone and Llantarnam Junction to Hafodyrynys. However, this did not happen and the rate increase imposed on the traffic to cover the longer journey

On the west side of the yards, Newport Pill's '42XX' 2–8–0T No.4276 is pictured on the Eastern Valleys line with a train of empties for Blaenavon Colliery on Thursday, 26th March 1959. Whilst the wagons forming the train were largely of steel designs, there were still a couple of wooden vehicles marshalled within it. The pannier tank standing against the water column on the left was possibly Canton's No.9759. This photograph was probably taken from the low viaduct that spanned the yards, and which road then cut through the Eastern Valleys embankment to the right of the photographer to join Coedygric Road, Griffithstown. The houses of Railway Terrace (later Station Road) form the backdrop.
S. RICKARD/J & J COLLECTION

Coedygric Junction (Eastern Valleys line), just to the north of Panteg & Griffithstown station, looking north in the later 1950s, with Pontypool Road's No.3717 shunting from Panteg Steelworks. On the right is Panteg & Coedygric Jct. box, with the old line to Pontypool Road station (still used by some passenger services) swinging to its right. This line also gave connections to most of the individual, central yards within the complex, and provided another running line that gave access to the eastern parts (this ran to East Jct.). Immediately beyond Panteg & Coedygric box, another Goods line ran underneath that for the station (etc.), connecting the main line (PC&N) at Panteg with the northerly yards.
RALPH CHARLES

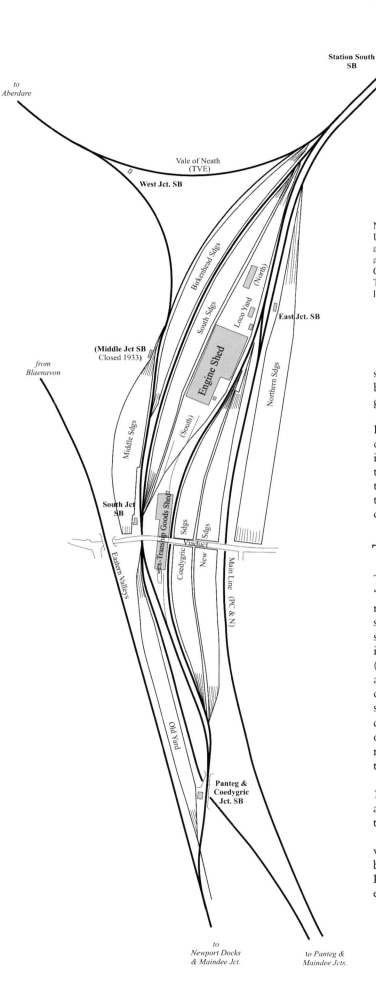

from Station

Station South SB

to Aberdare

Vale of Neath (TVE)

West Jct. SB

Birkenhead Sdgs

(North)

Loco Yard

South Sdgs

East Jct. SB

(Middle Jct SB Closed 1933)

from Blaenavon

Engine Shed

Northern Sdgs

Middle Sdgs

(South)

South Jct SB

Ex-Tranship Goods Shed

Coedygric Sdgs

New Sdgs

Viaduct

Main Line (PC & N)

Eastern Valleys

Old Yard

Panteg & Coedygric Jct. SB

to Newport Docks & Maindee Jct.

to Panteg & Maindee Jcts.

YARDS & JUNCTIONS, PONTYPOOL ROAD, c.1950

NOTES
Up to the interwar period, the Goods Running Loop between East and Panteg & Coedygric Junctions passed between the Coedygric and New Sidings, but was then diverted to run to the west of the Coedygric, as shown here.
That shown between Middle and Station South boxes was a single line, nominally for running in the Up direction.

soon prompted the NCB to provide an underground link between the two pits, whereupon the traffic passed underground.

It was a shame that such a historically important yard as Pontypool Road should have ended in such chaotic circumstances. Large sections of the yard were taken out of use in 1966, those sidings left operational being used mostly for the storage of condemned wagons and also for engineers' traffic. Unlike some other yard closures, where sections needed to be retained for ongoing traffic purposes, Pontypool Road died completely.

Tranship and Local Goods

To the west of the Birkenhead Sidings was the original goods 'transfer' (Tranship) depot of the 1860s, with two through roads and deck access between them, and a small group of shorter goods yard sidings for storage. The depot handled small consignment traffic, this being transferred from various incoming wagons to form an outgoing load for a particular (local) rail destination where it had not been feasible to load a full wagon between origin and destination. It also sent its daily outbound wagons (with consignments from local stations) to other tranship depots for the same purpose. Later diagrams of the area show a small goods yard south of the original station on the down side, which may have been responsible for delivering local traffic passed there from the tranship depot.

A new, larger Goods Tranship depot was opened around 1902 alongside the yard's South Junction, with limited road access seemingly across the Coedygric Jct. route and under the Eastern Valley line into Coedygric Road.

Virtually all of the tranship traffic would, however, remain within the confines of the shed, being moved manually between wagons for onwards movement. Traffic received for Pontypool itself and its environs would have been taken to either the Pontypool Road goods depot or to Crane Street for

106

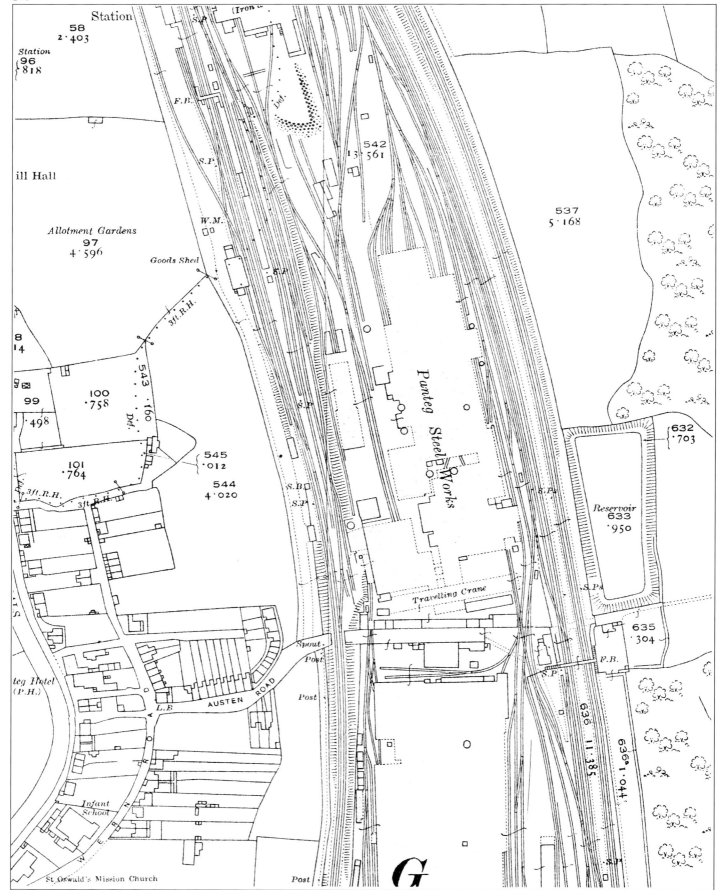

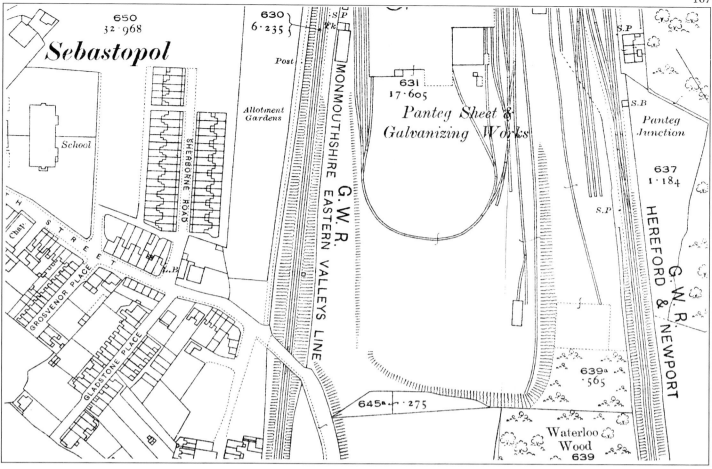

delivery. In 1929, Pontypool Road Tranship Depot connected with many other tranship depots daily as follows:

Inbound from	Outbound to
Birmingham	Abergavenny
Brecon	Birmingham
Bridgend	Bristol
Bristol	Caerphilly
Cardiff (Newtown)	Cardiff
Chester	Chester
Gloucester	Gloucester
Hereford	Hereford
Llanelly	Llanelly
Merthyr	Market Drayton
Neath	Merthyr
Nelson & Llancaiach	Newport
Newport High St.	Paddington
Newport Dock St.	Pengam (Glam.)
Pengam (Glam.)	Pontypridd
Pontypridd	Wolverhampton
Reading	Worcester
Shrewsbury	
Whitland	
Worcester	

Whilst nearly all of the depots handling tranship traffic were also goods sheds working with originating and terminating consignments, Pontypool Road Tranship Depot was unique on the Great Western in being maintained as a tranship point alone.

The Tranship shed served local stations on surrounding routes by rail (station truck, etc.), delivering and collecting

traffic depending upon the origin or destination of a consignment. For example, a small consignment from Cardiff to Penpergwm would be delivered via Pontypool Road Tranship, but one from Chester to Penpergwm would route via Hereford Tranship. Traffic from Penpergwm would be similarly routed, northbound consignments via Hereford and southbound via Pontypool Road. The routes served by Pontypool Road were:

Route	Balanced with
Hereford to Pontypool Rd (and Golden Valley Line)	Hereford
Pontypool Road to Chepstow (via STJ or Monmouth)	Newport High St or Gloucester
Caerleon to Pontypool Rd. or Pontypool (Clarence St.)	Newport High St
Pontypool Road to Neath (and branches, except Eastern and Western Valleys)	Neath

The use of the shed as a tranship centre ceased in 1932 as the Great Western drastically rationalised the arrangements, with the original 67 (mostly small) centres throughout the system being reduced to just nine: these were at Paddington, Birmingham, Wolverhampton, Chester, Newport, Cardiff, Llanelly, Bristol and Plymouth (the last-named soon being removed from the list, leaving eight). Newport now handled Pontypool's tranship traffic, with Crane Street delivering or collecting by road.

Continued on page 126

By May 1964, when this view was taken of the south end of the shed, Pontypool Road had amassed its largest ever allocation of 'Halls' and 'Granges'. Long-term resident No.6840 *Hazeley Grange* features at the head of the line of engines, with a 'Hall' and Stanier '8F' also visible with '56XXs', another '8F', panniers and a '41XX' across the picture. The eastern part of Pontypool may be seen at the foot of the hill towards the left-hand edge of the picture, with the loop from the yards to West Junction on the Vale of Neath before it, in the middle distance. The pair of shunting trucks in the foreground were marked 'Pontypool Road'; in the war years, the yards had five allocated.

ROGER HOLMES/HUGH DAVIES

PONTYPOOL ROAD SHED

The first locomotive shed in the Pontypool area was the MR& CC depot at Coedygric, opened in July 1852. Located just to the east of Coedygric Jct, it was a 'sector' design, with six or seven short roads radiating from a turntable, two of which terminated in a small shed. Another engine shed was provided at Pontypool Crane Street station (MR&CC), opened in October 1854.

At Coedygric, it seems probable that engines from both the MR&CC and the NA&H shared facilities. Its short-comings were obviously clear by the mid-1860s, when a proposal was made to replace it with a larger shed situated in the area between Coedygric Jct. and the south end of the passenger station at Pontypool Road. This was approved by the Board in the summer of 1864.

The new engine shed at Pontypool Road was opened in 1865 to replace the Coedygric depot, which was then closed. It is again possible that both the GWR (who by this time had amalgamated with the West Midland, the successor to the NA&H) and the Monmouthshire company again shared facilities, though the latter concern's main depot was only eight miles away, at Newport (Bolt St.). It may have been that the shed was constructed in two parts, as in January 1870 the Board directed the 'erection of an engine shed for twenty engines' to be commenced at once.

Pontypool Road shed comprised two very different sections – a roundhouse of twenty dead-end roads off the turntable at the north end, with a through road over the turntable leading from the north end yard into the attached second part, an eight-road shed with seven lines stopblocked at their northern ends.

A coal stage was provided in the north yard, with water, inspection and office facilities around the site.

By 1901, the first year for which comprehensive records are available, the depot contained a fascinating collection of goods engine designs dating back to 1855, and probably due to the fact that a large percentage of its trains ran to the north, it was embraced within the Northern Division of the GWR. In 1901, the engines allocated ranged from a member of the Gooch standard gauge First Goods Lot 0-6-0s (No.66), of the '57' class, through the Gooch '79' class and others to the Dean 'Standard Goods', with a total allocation of 103 engines. It was a principal depot, largely for the movement of coal traffic to the north, and to service all the local industrial concerns and branch lines in the area. The 1901 allocation was:

Class		Engines
4-4-0	'Duke'	3258 *King Arthur*
	'3521'	3545
2-4-0	'3232'	3235
	'717'	719, 720, 724
0-6-0	'57'	66
	'79'	79, 80, 81, 82, 84, 87, 89,122
	'131'	311, 315
	'322'	328, 329, 331, 332, 333, 334, 335, 336, 337,
	('Beyer')	338, 339, 340, 341, 350, 351, 352, 353, 354,
		355, 356, 357, 358, 359
	'Standard'	394, 498, 508, 513, 515, 661, 667, 777
	(Armstrong)	797, 884, 1083
	'2301'(Dean)	2324, 2375, 2424, 2528, 2541, 2554, 2568

0-6-0ST &	'119'	120, 121, 123, 124, 125, 128, 130
0-6-0T	'850'	1948, 1954, 2009
	'1016'	1019, 1026, 1041, 1059, 1065, 1069
	'1076'	1139, 1143, 1152, 1183, 1245, 1261, 1611,
	('Buffalo')	1614, 1659, 1660
	'1661'	1669, 1675
	'1813'	1847
	'1854'	1724, 1857
	'2021'	2033, 2034, 2057, 2072, 2073
0-4-2T	'3571'	3576

The presence of the 4-4-0 'Duke' and a rebuilt '3521' class, plus 2-4-0s, indicates the presence of a small number of main-line passenger duties, and the two 4-4-0 classes were recorded on Hereford and Birmingham trains.

Northern freights to Birkenhead, etc. would have been very largely handled by the 0-6-0 tender engine fleet, though the '1076' ('Buffalo') class were known to have worked many long-distance coal trains, often double-headed, with appropriate stops for water and re-coaling.

Other known duties included '1016', '1076' and '3571' classes on VoN passenger trains to Aberdare or Swansea.

By the end of 1910, most of the old goods engines had been withdrawn, and the 'Aberdare' class had made its presence felt at the depot with eight allocated, probably for working the main turns to Birkenhead. There were still, however, five members of the '322' (or 'Beyer') class allocated, and ten 'Standard Goods', plus a few examples of other veteran GWR designs. For main-line passenger and mixed traffic work, there were four 'Bulldogs', which may indicate that the 1901 allocation of 4-4-0 and 2-4-0 engines were their predecessors. The depot was still predominantly a freight depot with a large local shunting and transfer workload in the marshalling yard, and serving the local works and branches.

Between the turn of the century and 1910, Pontypool Road played host to a variety of 4-4-0 classes, with 'Dukes' between 1900-08 (varying between one and four, the maximum in 1903); a 'Badminton' between 1903 and 1906; a 'County' from 1906 to 1909; and the ubiquitous 'Bulldogs' from 1901, the allocation rising to three or four between 1905 and 1910. The varying allocation doubtless reflected the vagaries of diagramming on the North & West, the 'County' allocation probably being made for a Shrewsbury duty.

The allocation at the end of 1910 was as follows (NB these numbers are before the renumbering of 28th December 1912):

4-4-0	'Bulldog'	3456 *Albany*, 3462 *Winnipeg*
		3702 *John G. Griffiths*, 3727
2-6-0	'Aberdare'	2601, 2604, 2605, 2628, 2638, 2644, 2662,
		2677
0-6-0	'79'	122
	'378'	476
	'Standard'	23, 438, 451, 611, 660, 667, 675, 688, 1095,
	Goods	1192, 1204
	'322' ('Beyer')	332, 336, 340, 341, 359
	'927' ('Coal')	927
	'2301' (Dean)	2364, 2376, 2419, 2524, 2566
2-4-0T	'Metro'	975
2-4-2T	'36XX'	3612
0-6-0T &	'119'	121, 129

0-6-0ST	'302'	309
	'655'	1775
	'850'	1984
	'1016'	1025, 1026, 1031, 1048
	'1076'	742, 745, 966, 1078, 1140, 1146, 1172, 1233,
	('Buffalo')	1246, 1254, 1255, 1276, 1566, 1574, 1599,
		1605, 1609, 1614, 1640, 1653
	'1854'	1708, 1726
	'2021'	2122, 2138, 2143, 2150
0-4-0ST	W. Cornwall	1391

Total 74 engines allocated

The early years of the second decade began quietly at the depot, marked only by the return of a 'Badminton' No. 4103 *Bessborough* in 1911, which was replaced by No. 4104 *Cambria* in June 1915 when the other went to Swindon Works, remaining until 1920. Trials were held with trains of coal for the British fleet to Grangemouth, considering the possibility of an impending war. These were held with 'Aberdare' and 'Standard Goods' engines, but hardly represented the state-of-the-art with other parts of the system running the newer '2800' class 2-8-0s, capable of taking up to a further twelve wagons more than the 'Aberdares' on the North & West route. When war was declared in August 1914, the fear became a reality with an Admiralty decision to avoid U-boat attack by conveying a proportion of the coal for the fleet, berthed in Scapa Flow, to Grangemouth (and other destinations) by rail instead of coaster. Pontypool Road had an allocation of 11 'Aberdares' and only one '28XX' (No. 2845). As experience was gained of the 'Aberdares' working through to Chester/ Warrington on the 'Jellicoe Special' coal trains, as the services were dubbed, the GWR were forced, either on their own volition or through Admiralty pressure, to transfer a fleet of '28XXs' to Pontypool Road to work these trains. Progressively during the first six months of 1915, '28XXs' were withdrawn from the main-line goods services out of London and transferred to Pontypool Road, so that by the end of June, that shed had 25 on their books, with an allocation of 26 at year's end. With 28 allocated at the start of 1917 and 1918, the number was increased with new engines during 1918 so that by the end of that year, the allocation stood at 32. With the cessation of hostilities, the demand for the services reduced, and then ceased, but at the beginning of 1920, Pontypool Road still had 19 '28XXs' and 11 'Aberdares' on their books. On the 'Jellicoes', the Pontypool Road crews had worked through to Chester/Warrington.

As to 4-4-0s, 'Atbaras' were first allocated to Pontypool Road in March 1917, with three allocated during 1917/8, reducing to two in 1919/20 then one until 1925, when the allocation ceased. 'Counties' also re-appeared in 1919 with first one, then 2/3 allocated between 1920-24, after which they varied between none and two until the final one, No. 3822 *County of Brecon* was withdrawn in 1933. 'Bulldogs' remained at the depot from 1910 until mid-1917, the allocation ranging between three and five, but in 1917 they were all transferred away and the depot's dependence on the class virtually ceased, with only one (or sometimes two) being allocated until 1948.

Also in 1919 came an event of major significance to Pontypool Road, with the progressive transfer to the depot of seven different 'Saints', though four were moved away after short stays. However, this set the trend for the future years when the depot maintained its allocation of three or four of the class. It was said that this allocation was a gesture on the part of GWR Directors for the depot's sterling work on the 'Jellicoes'. The allocation was no doubt the result of dexterous manipulation of the North & West timetable and diagrams. The original allocation included No. 2900 *William Dean* for 3 months, no doubt a prized possession.

Additional sidings were added to the north yard to accommodate more engines and loco coal wagons.

In January 1920, there were still five 'Standard Goods' left at Pontypool Road, and one class '322' (or 'Beyer'), as well as some 'Dean Goods'. The main-line goods fleet had by now been largely modernised with 'Aberdares' and '2800' classes; the allocation at that time stood at 82 as follows:

4-6-0	'Saint'	2918 *Saint Catherine*, 2954 *Tockenham Court*,
		2974 *Lord Barrymore*
4-4-0	'County'	3826 *County of Flint*
	'Badminton'	4104 *Cambria*
	'Atbara'	4121 *Baden Powell*, 4145 *Dunedin*
2-8-0	'28XX'	2805, 2808, 2810, 2812, 2816, 2824, 2829,
		2837, 2839, 2842, 2843, 2851, 2857
2-6-0	'Aberdare'	2621, 2629, 2630, 2638, 2640, 2665, 2668,
		2677
	'43XX'	4320, 4324, 4326, 4379, 5321
0-6-0	'322' ('Beyer')	329
	'Standard	395, 792, 1083, 1099, 1197
	Goods'	
	'2301'(Dean)	2362, 2386, 2439, 2562, 2568, 2573, 2577
0-6-0ST	'302'	304, 309
& 0-6-0T	'633'	639
	'850'	1915, 1984
	'1016'	1056
	'1076'	732, 1173, 1245, 1261, 1278, 1288, 1561,
	('Buffalo')	1572, 1573, 1574, 1595, 1599, 1614, 1620,
		1659
	'1661'	1672, 1682
	'1854'	1766, 1797
	'2021'	2035, 2047, 2117, 2133, 2136, 2154
	'2721'	2750, 2763, 2791
2-4-0T	'Metro'	632, 1414

Various 4-4-0s were based at Pontypool Road during the 1920s. The last 'Badminton' at the depot, No. 4104 *Cambria*, left at the beginning of 1920, at which time there were two 'Atbaras' allocated, one of which remained until 1925. Until that year there were three 'Counties' allocated, but this then dropped to two or less with none based there from mid-1928 to January 1931, when one was again allocated, remaining until April 1933. A 'Flower', No. 4165 *Narcissus*, was allocated in November 1921, remaining until 1924 when it was replaced by No. 4151 *Calceolaria*, which remained until the end of 1927, when she was withdrawn. By now, 'Bulldogs' had become conspicuous by their absence from the allocation, with none allocated between mid-1917 and 1921, and during the 1920s decade there was just one allocated in 1921 and 1925 to 1928. The newly arrived 'Saints' maintained their presence during the 'twenties with between three and six

A view of the south end of the shed in the 1930s, with two 'Aberdares' and a 'Pannier' on display. The 'Aberdares' were Nos. 2667, which was at Pontypool Road or Aberdare sheds from 1925 to 1937, and 2672, from Cardiff, but Pontypool Road briefly in 1934/5, prior to withdrawal. The pannier, Pontypool Road's No. 8712, was present there from new in 1931 until 1943.
JOHN HODGE

allocated, during what was probably one of the heyday periods of the depot.

By 1930, the allocation had fallen to 72 engines. All the veteran goods 0-6-0s were gone, and the main-line freight was completely worked by the 'Aberdares', '28XXs', 'RODs' and '43XXs', possibly with the involvement of some of the 'Saints' on the faster work. Details of the allocation are:

4-6-0	'Saint'	2948 *Stackpole Court*, 2973 *Robins Bolitho*, 2988 *Rob Roy*, 2989 *Talisman*
2-8-0	'28XX'	2814, 2821, 2822, 2823, 2826, 2829, 2835, 2839, 2840, 2866, 2868
	'ROD'	3037, 3038
2-6-0	'Aberdare'	2605, 2652, 2655, 2667, 2669
	'43XX'	4350, 4363, 4366, 4393, 6365
0-6-0	'2301'(Dean)	2307, 2523, 2536
2-8-0T	'42XX'	4243, 4249
2-6-2T	'45XX'	4597
0-6-2T	'56XX'	6651, 6656, 6666
0-6-0ST	'633'	639
& 0-6-0T	'645'	90
	'850'	1931
	'1076' ('Buffalo')	744, 753, 958, 963, 1585, 1620, 1621, 1640, 1656
	'1501'	1534, 1535
	'1813'	1838, 1849
	'1854'	1721, 1730
	'2021'	2021, 2034, 2035, 2080, 2094, 2132, 2133, 2140, 2141, 2160
	'2721'	2724, 2749, 2788
	'57XX'	5728
2-4-0T	'Metro'	456, 981
Steam Rail Motors		76, 77

In 1932, two ex-Taff Vale class 'A' 0-6-2Ts, Nos. 335 and 385, were allocated to Pontypool Road for local shunting and for banking to Llanvihangel. In 1935, No. 335 was replaced by No. 349, and the two remained at Pontypool until the mid-1950s when both were moved away, to Barry and Canton. They did not apparently enjoy a very high reputation at the depot, though were much liked elsewhere.

The allocation and work of Pontypool's engines for March 1938 was as follows:

Class	Passr	Gds	Shunt	Bank	Pilot	Spl	Allocation
'Saint'	2	-	-	-	-	1	2922, 2940, 2952
'Grange'	-	2	-	-	-	-	6819, 6830
'Bulldog'	1	-	-	-	-	-	3391
'72XX'	-	5	-	-	-	-	7206, 7233, 7235
'28XX'	-	7	-	-	-	1	2801, 2802, 2804, 2821 2853, 2885
'ROD'	-	1	-	-	-	1	3018, 3023, 3037
'42XX'	-	2	-	-	-	-	4264, 4280
'43XX'	-	4	-	-	-	1	4303, 5310, 5347, 5355, 6325, 6333, 6356, 7321
'26XX'	-	3	-	-	-	-	-
'45XX'	3	1	-	-	-	-	4504, 4533, 4597, 5517
'56XX'	-	3	-	-	-	-	5649, 6634, 6636, 6666, 6687
TV 0-6-2T	-	-	-	2	-	-	349, 385
'2301'	-	-	-	-	1	1	2470
0-6-0Ts	4	4	$\frac{1}{2}$	1	$1\frac{1}{2}$	1	850: 2009
							1813: 1847
							1854: 1705, 1722, 1730
							2021: 2034, 2041, 2077, 2094, 2160
							2721: 2749
							74XX: 7402

'57XX'	2	2	1	1	2½	-	3717, 3726, 3730, 7720, 7747, 7768, 8712, 8724, 8776
'64XX'	3	-	-	-	-	-	Auto: 6400, 6424, 6429, 6432, 6438
'2021'	3	-	-	-	-	-	Auto: 2080, 2117, 2132, 2159
'48XX'	-	-	-	-	-	-	Auto: 4822, 4823
Diesel RC (1)	-	-	-	-	-	-	14, 16

As usual, there were some clerical discrepancies between the turns and the actual allocation; the 'shortfalls' seen above were generally covered by other suitable classes, or by loans from other sheds. The 'half' turns related to 24-hour duties, where '1½' engines were effectively required to cover the ongoing work.

The transitional nature of the allocation between the old guard and the new was very evident, with 11 of the older-style panniers still allocated, mostly of the '2021' class, and ten of the newer design. There were supposedly still two 'Aberdares' at the shed, though there was a temporary absence between October 1936 and January 1940, when a pair of condemned engines were reprieved and sent to Pontypool Road. Though no 'Halls' had as yet arrived, two of the newer 'Granges' had been allocated in 1937 for fast freight work. Three of the new '72XX' heavy freight engines were now allocated, and were used among other routes on the Ebbw Vale turns. As can be seen, there was a surplus of auto engines and diesel cars to the duties.

Facing a sister engine, 'ROD' 2–8–0 No. 3018 is seen here on shed at Pontypool Road during September 1936. At this time, she was allocated to Pontypool with three others of her class, having recently been transferred in from Hereford during the preceding January. In this period, the class were recorded on goods services between Pontypool Road and Aberdare, Coleham, and Oxley, and on through Newport & Banbury trains.
RAY HINTON ARCHIVE

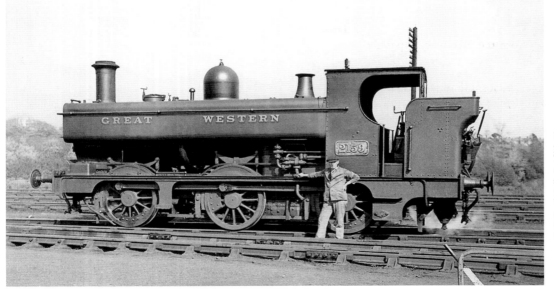

Pontypool Road's '2021' No. 2159 pictured on shed on 10th May 1936. The engine was recorded as being auto-fitted at this time, and four were supplied to work three passenger turns, visiting Monmouth and the Eastern Valleys lines. In addition, six non-auto engines were used in the yards, and on freights to Monmouth, Panteg and Cwmbran.
F.K. DAVIES/ GW TRUST

In 1940, two 'Saints' and a 'Bulldog' were still on the books, and also a new class to the depot, a '3150' class 2-6-2T No. 3161, which had had a very chequered career in terms of repair and may have been allocated to Pontypool in 1939 to have a close eye kept on her. No 3161's stay was not long, and after yet another works visit to Caerphilly in 1940, she was moved to Canton. Six of the new '64XX' auto-fitted pannier tanks were now allocated for working the Eastern Valley and other branch services, plus the two '48XX' 0-4-2Ts, whilst all the old auto '2021s' were still in evidence, working on the branches until at least the middle part of the war. With 80 engines allocated, Pontypool Road was still a prime GWR depot.

The decline in the older engines was more marked by 1950, by which time the depot had acquired the new BR description '86G', replacing the former Great Western PPRD'. There were still four of the '2021' class panniers at work there, but the declining 'Saint' and 'Bulldog' classes had all been transferred away. The largest engines now at the depot were the four 'Halls'. Two 'WD' 2-8-0s had joined the fleet of heavy main-line freight engines. The allocation was as follows:

4-6-0	'Hall'	4912 *Berrington Hall*, 4932 *Hatherton Hall*, 4933 *Himley Hall*, 5975 *Winslow Hall*
	'Grange'	6875 *Hindford Grange*
2-8-0	'28XX'	2800, 2801, 2802, 2811, 2813, 2845, 2862, 2864, 2884, 2888, 2893, 3822, 3826, 3828, 3862
	'ROD'	3012, 3018, 3023, 3038, 3040, 3042, 3044
	'WD'	90268, 90563
2-6-0	'43XX'	4303, 5355, 6333, 6370
0-6-0	'2301'	2385
2-8-2T	'72XX'	7206, 7233, 7234, 7235
2-8-0T	'42XX'	4271
2-6-2T	'51XX'	4121, 4130, 4131, 4135, 4138, 4158
	'45XX'	4533, 4541, 4593, 5516, 5532
0-6-2T	'56XX'	6636, 6663, 6687
	TV 'A'	349, 385
0-6-0T	'2021'	2021, 2035, 2094, 2117
	'57XX'	3628, 3651, 3690, 3692, 3717, 3730, 3778, 4611, 4639, 4642, 4668, 5728, 5768, 5792, 6742, 7724, 7740, 8716, 8755, 8788, 9650, 9797
	'64XX'	6400, 6403, 6424, 6429, 6430, 6432
	'74XX'	7426
0-4-2T	'14XX'	1422
	'58XX'	5818
Diesel Rail Car		W30

One of the main passenger duties was to take over the 9.25 a.m. Manchester to Swansea from the incoming Longsight engine and work this to Cardiff, returning with the 4.40 p.m. Cardiff to Hereford, a turn entrusted to a 4-6-0, 2-6-0 or even a 2-6-2 tank. In the latter 1950s, the turn became the province of Grange No. 6840 after its release from Swindon, following which it was kept in pristine condition and worked this turn over a considerable period. Pontypool Road 4-6-0s and 2-6-0s invariably turned up working Summer Saturday trains over considerable distances, both off outgoing freight turns and taking over Friday night trains from Manchester to the West of England at Pontypool Road. Their '41XXs', which worked mostly on the Vale of Neath, covered excursions to Barry Island (from Blaenavon and Pontypool Road) on summer weekends and bank holidays, often with ten-coach loads, and also football excursions to Cardiff in winter.

By the mid 'fifties, the '2021s', Dean Goods and 'RODs' had been withdrawn, and the TV 'As' transferred to the Cardiff Valleys, whilst many of the early '28XXs' and '43XXs' would soon be scrapped. Branch line closures ended the allocation of auto-fitted engines.

Three 'Halls' were working variously between Bristol, Cardiff, Hereford and Shrewsbury with passenger, parcels and perishable traffic, with two 'Granges' on similar duties.

Freight duties were better documented, with four 'Halls' and 'Granges' on fast services to Worcester, Saltney and Bordesley. The '28XXs' handled heavier trains from the yard to Coton Hill, Saltney, Croes Newydd, Stourbridge Jct., Tyseley and Cardiff, whilst the '43XXs' worked to Coton Hill, Saltney and Tyseley. 'RODs' were scheduled to Oxley Sdgs., Hinksey (Oxford), Bristol and Severn Tunnel Jct., 'WDs' on the 'Control Order' special turns, and LMR '7Fs' to Shrewsbury yards.

Overall, duties in the late 1950s were to similar destinations, though with a '72XX' on trips to Ebbw Vale and Roath Sdgs., and a '56XX' to Stormstown and Aberbargoed.

The dieselisation of the West of England in the late 1950s threw up many spare 4-6-0s, from which Pontypool Road benefited from 1958 onwards, especially with 'Granges'. The combined effect of these features produced the following summary allocation throughout the 1950s and early 1960s of engines performing similar duties, before the depot closed:

		1950	1955	1959	1960	1962	1963
Main Line	'28XX'	15	8	11	13	11	8
Freight &	'WD'	2	3	3	1	-	-
Passenger	'43XX'	4	2	8	7	4	4
	'Hall'	4	5	6	13	11	9
	'Grange'	1	4	6	8	10	10
	Total	*33*	*29*	*34*	*42*	*36*	*31*
Shunting &	'57XX'	22	28	27	27	25	16
Tripping	'2021'	4	-	-	-	-	-
	TV 'A'/						
	'84XX'	2	-	-	2	3	2
	'74XX'	1	1	-	-	-	-
	Total	*29*	*29*	*27*	*29*	*28*	*18*
Local Passenger	'51XX'	6	3	2	2	2	2
& Freight	'61XX'	-	-	-	-	1	2
	'56XX'	3	8	8	11	12	4
	Total	*9*	*11*	*10*	*13*	*15*	*8*
Branch Auto	'64XX'	6	5	3	-	-	-
	DRC	1	-	-	-	-	-
	Total	*7*	*5*	*3*	-	-	-
Branch Freight/	'42XX'	1	2	1	-	-	-
Banking	'72XX'	4	7	8	7	6	7
	LMR	-	3	3	1	-	-
	Total	*5*	*12*	*12*	*8*	*6*	*7*

In 1963, Pontypool Road's engines were still scheduled on freight duties to many locations. Eight 'Halls' ran variously to Shrewsbury, Saltney, Yarnton and Bristol, and seven 'Granges' were on three turns to Abercwmboi, Saltney and Crewe; Worcester, Crewe, Oxley, Cardiff and Saltney; and Saltney again. The '28XXs' were utilised on turns to Stourbridge Jct., Croes Newydd, and Oxley, with '43XXs' to Worcester.

Pontypool Road depot closed in May 1965.

The south end of the straight-road shed, looking north, in May 1964. A single water column served the eight roads, though narrow spacing between the tracks doubtless prevented a more generous supply system. The siding to the left, on which a large number of engines may be seen, was connected to the shed's trackwork, and not to the adjacent South Sidings, and was stated in the 1920s to have the capacity for 43 wagons; over the years, it seems to have been used more for engines than wagons, though one photograph does show a couple of the latter present at its north end, perhaps relating to the coal stage.

D.K. JONES COLLECTION

Machynlleth's class '4MT' 4-6-0 No.75004 was some way from home, pictured on the long siding in October 1962, but it may have been 'borrowed' and worked in from Shrewsbury. The class were, however, also occasionally to be seen at Pontypool, as Worcester had a couple of examples. No.2887 on the right was from Cardiff East Dock, which shed had just become Cardiff's refuge for the remaining steam locomotives working there, with the adoption of Canton for diesels.

D.K. JONES COLLECTION

No.4990 *Clifton Hall* is seen here being prepared at the south end for a northbound working, with the low sun indicating around noon one winter's day, in the mid-1950s. This engine was at Pontypool Road for four years from October 1952, and may have been working the early afternoon freight to Harlescott Sidings, Shrewsbury, which was a 'Hall' turn. No.6876 *Kingsland Grange* can be seen to the right – this was a St. Philip's Marsh engine in this period. The Eastern Valleys line can just be seen behind the tender, in the background, on its embankment.
DEREK POTTON/TRANSPORT TREASURY

The massive bulk of the '72XXs' is well illustrated in this view of Pontypool Road's No.7210, standing on the long siding that ran around the west side of the shed, adjacent to South Sidings, on 10th May 1964. This engine was very much of the eastern section of South Wales, with a long initial allocation to Severn Tunnel Jct. (1934–50) followed by spells at Canton, Ebbw Jct., and from August 1958, Pontypool Road. They were used more on local trips by this time, with 'Halls', 'Granges' and '28XXs' scheduled for the longer-distance workings.
D.K. JONES COLLECTION

Another view of the south end on 11th July 1958, showing the yard goods/shunting signals and more of the engines on shed, including Aberdare's No.8444, and a '43XX' to the left. The twin roofs of the eight-road section are seen here, all being dead-end apart from the third from the right (on which No.8444 was standing), which ran through to the turntable in the large, northern section of the shed. The road immediately to the left of the bracket signal ran around the shed to link with the Up Goods line. H.C. CASSERLEY

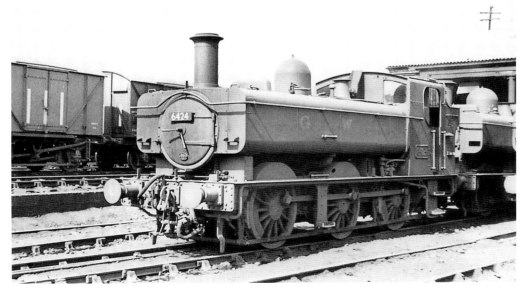

On my first ever trip to Pontypool Road one day in the summer of 1950 (at the ripe old age of 12½), I was taken round the shed by my uncle, who was a Carriage & Wagon Examiner there. At the back (south) end of the shed we found Ebbw Jct. 'Saint' No.2979 *Quentin Durward*, a Newport engine since 1941, but soon to be withdrawn (at the end of January 1951). On the day, the Longsight turn, which had recently started, was worked by rebuilt 'Patriot' No.45530 *Sir Frank Ree*, which was also briefly on shed at that time.

JOHN HODGE

Still in its final GWR livery, No.6424 is pictured outside the south end of the shed on Sunday, 15th April 1951. The engine was one of six at Pontypool Road (the others being 6400, 6403, 6429, 6430 and 6432) for auto work on the Eastern Valleys line, starting with the 4.15 a.m. empty to Panteg, for Blaenavon; and over the TVE, commencing with the 6.40 a.m. to Nelson & Llancaiach. They also ran to Usk, and Abergavenny.

B.W.L. BROOKSBANK/
INITIAL PHOTOGRAPHICS

'45XX' No.4541 at the south end of the shed on 6th April 1952. The engine had been at Pontypool Road since November 1947, and would remain there for another six months before moving westwards to Whitland. No.4541 had been in South Wales since 1928, and would remain there until withdrawal in 1955. Throughout the region, the class was very much associated with main line and branch passenger duties, and this was also the case with Pontypool Road's engines, although there was invariably at least one goods turn in the four allocated to the five engines.
L.R. FREEMAN/
TRANSPORT TREASURY

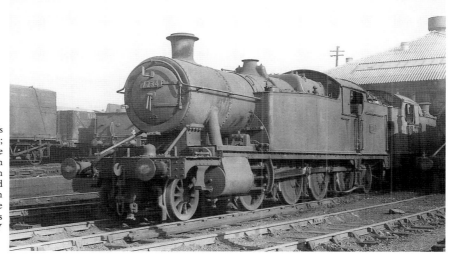

Pontypool Road had four '72XX' 2–8–2Ts for three goods turns in the summer of 1953; one of these, No.7234, was recorded at the shed on Sunday, 13th September. A known '72XX' weekday evening duty at this time ran from Little Mill to Cardiff Goods. The shed at Pontypool Road was hemmed in between goods running lines or sidings, with the wagons to the left standing in South Sidings yard.
NORMAN PREEDY

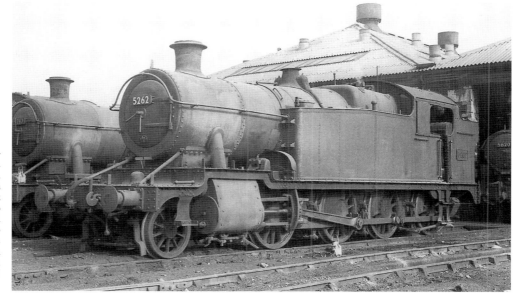

'42XX' 2–8–0T No.5262 outside the straight-road shed on Sunday, 13th September 1953. This engine was from Severn Tunnel Junction, whose '42XXs' mostly ran out along the main line to Margam, Landore, Swansea East Dock and Llandilo Jct. (Llanelly), but there were also three or four local trips daily to Pontypool Road, doubtless with a '42XX' from time to time. Behind No.5262 is Pontypool's No.5620, and alongside is No.5210 from Swansea East Dock, probably having run in with a goods via Aberdare.
RAY HINTON

A selection of engines in the roundhouse section on 3rd August 1964, with Pannier No.9650 (Pontypool) '2251' 0–6–0 No.2287 (Hereford), and 2–8–2T No.7210 (Pontypool) in view. Built around 1879, the roundhouse contained eighteen storage roads off the turntable, as well as the two through roads, but some sources give the former figure in later years as twenty.   R.K. BLENCOWE COLLECTION

Cardiff East Dock's 'Castle' No.5092 *Tresco Abbey* is seen on shed at the straight-road building on Saturday, 1st June 1963, ready turned to make a return trip. It was late afternoon, and the engine may have been waiting to take the Cardiff portion of the 3.5 p.m. Manchester onwards from Pontypool Road. *Tresco Abbey* would be withdrawn from traffic the following month after a 25-year career at Gloucester, Worcester, Old Oak, Bath Road and, finally, in August 1960, Cardiff.
NORMAN PREEDY

Grimy 2–8–0T No.4295, without shedplate, standing before the back (south) end of the shed on 3rd August 1964, with part of the original stonework of the shed wall visible to its right. The engine had only recently been transferred in from Tondu, which had closed, and survived until December, when there were a mere 13 locomotives shedded at Pontypool Road. Pontypool Road shed itself closed in May 1965.
R.K. BLENCOWE COLLECTION

Oxley 'Grange' No.6851 *Hurst Grange* is pictured at the south end with Pontypool Road's '56XX' No.6685 and '57XX' No.4642 on Sunday, 14th October 1962. The 'Grange' duties northwards out of Pontypool Road in this period were to Shrewsbury (for Crewe), Saltney and Worcester, and it is probable that the last was the destination for this engine on its way back to Oxley. The '56XXs' at this time were scheduled for duties to Cardiff, Stormstown Jct. (Abercynon), Aberbargoed, Aberdare High Level, and Dowlais Central with ICI tanks.
D.K. JONES COLLECTION

A May 1964 view of the roundhouse, looking south over the through track leading across the turntable into the earlier, straight-road shed beyond. Engines on the left are 0–6–0T No.8495 (Pontypool), 'Hall' No.4976 *Warfield Hall* (Oxford) and 2–8–2T No.7201 (Pontypool), with more panniers visible in the gloom ahead. The turntable was a 55ft unit, sufficient to comfortably accommodate 'Halls', 'Granges' and '28XXs', and 'Castles' at a pinch, though not 'Kings', which would have had to use a suitable triangle, or run to Newport.
ROGER HOLME CTY. HUGH DAVIES

An atmospheric portrait of Newton Abbot 'Grange' No.6814 *Enborne Grange* in the roundhouse, along with Pontypool Road's '57XX' No.3717, on Tuesday, 4th September 1956. At this time, Newton's mixed traffic 4–6–0s regularly worked to Cardiff or Shrewsbury in the summer months on passenger trains, and to Cardiff throughout the year on a freight turn, but also to Pontypool Road with the 9.5 a.m. Paignton to Manchester on peak summer Saturdays; on this occasion, the train was taken onwards to Shrewsbury by a Chester 'Hall'. Perhaps a defect had prevented its prompt return to the West.

D.K. JONES COLLECTION

122

The north end of the shed, also on 11th July 1958, with a 'Grange' head-down for working south, its smokebox against an '8F' inside the structure, and two '56XXs' on the left, the leading one No.5638. There were three roads leading into the interior, the centre one of which ran through to the central turntable, the outer two again being dead-end. The elevated coal stage road extension is seen on the right.   H.C. CASSERLEY

'56XX' No.6653 at Pontypool Road Loco's north yard c.1957, with an '86G' shedplate. The shed had around nine of the engines at this time, for seven turns, primarily goods. One known duty was to Stormstown Jct. (Abercynon) and Rhondda Fach Jct. (Porth) with a morning freight, and to Aberbargoed on an evening goods duty. In February 1958, the engine moved on to Aberdare, and the following year further west to Llanelly.   NORMAN PREEDY

Pontypool Road's '72XX' No.7220, seen in the northern side of the loco yard, with the water tank behind, probably in the late 1950s. The roundhouse shed features to the left, and wagons can be seen on the section of elevated coal road beyond the coal stage, which was off to the right. On the right of the picture 'Enwheels' open wagon No. DW 274 was for the carriage of 'Loco Wheels Only', branded for 'Pontypool Rd'. J. DAVENPORT/INITIAL PHOTOGRAPHICS

Pontypool Road 'Pannier' No.4639, pictured outside the pump room/water tank in the Loco northern yard on 3rd August 1964. This engine went new to the shed in January 1943, and was one of the last engines there, being moved away (to Cardiff East Dock) in May 1965, at Pontypool Road's closure. By this time, the yard closure was effectively imminent, and few – if any – diesel shunter replacements were to be seen. R.K. BLENCOWE

No.4958 *Priory Hall* and No.5322 were both transferred to Pontypool Road shed in late 1959, and each remained there until mid-1964. The two are seen here on the ash roads at the north end, with a steam crane clearing away deposits.

DEREK POTTON/TRANSPORT TREASURY

The throat of the straight-road shed, looking south on 20th May 1959, with Shrewsbury Coleham's class '5MT' 4–6–0 No.73037 in the foreground. This view gives a rare sight of the replacement (c.1902) transship shed alongside South Junction, to the left of the engine, which was 'bisected' by the viaduct that ran east-west across the southern part of the yards (and can just be made out to the left of the shed). The shed was closed as a tranship centre c. 1932 as part of the rationalisation of that system.
D.K. JONES COLLECTION

Duffryn Yard '28XX' No.2813 standing alongside the ash shelter, north Loco yard, on Sunday, 14th September 1952. Duffryn Yard's turns for larger engines were mainly '42XXs' or '72XXs' from Margam yard, but there were two turns for its three '28XXs' at this time, one of which involved the Mondays-only 7.40 a.m. Little Mill Jct. to Briton Ferry, which may have been this engine's return working.
RAY HINTON

Pontypool Road was home to a diesel railcar from March 1936, when No.14 was utilised for branch/main line trips to Monmouth, Chepstow and Severn Tunnel Jct., and in the other direction over the main line to Newport, a daily turn of around 212 miles. No.30 drifted in and out of Pontypool Road from September 1942, though was more permanently settled there from 1946. She is seen here on shed on 14th September 1952, when her duties were largely confined to the four daily round trips to Monmouth, a total mileage of around 145. RAY HINTON

Continued from page 107

The small goods yard provided on the Down side near Pontypool Road station, opposite the later Station South box, comprised a small goods shed, some 30ft in length, containing a 1-ton crane, on a siding with a capacity of 24 wagons. Behind was a short siding to hold ten wagons, with a 10-ton yard crane between it and the shed road. At the rear of the yard was a siding for five wagons, serving a 57ft loading bank, and an end-loading 'carriage landing' at the buffer stops. This yard handled local small consignments (possibly only received from the tranship depot) and mileage traffic. It closed in 1930, when its function would have been taken over by Crane Street Goods. However, facilities were probably retained for domestic coal traffic.

The goods handling facilities at Pontypool Road warranted a Goods Agent, whose staff worked largely in the Transfer shed, and at the small goods depot to the south of the station. The Agent's staff in 1929 were:

Chief Clerk	1
Clerks:	
Inwards	2
Outwards	1
Shed Foremen	2
Checkers	5
Loaders	2
Porters	24

There were also 4 horses and 7 horse-drawn vehicles at the goods depot, possibly serving locations to the east, and possible movements to Crane Street which probably handled traffic for the town and its environs.

The Zonal system, introduced in the postwar era, made Newport the main railhead, with sub-railheads at Pontypool (Crane Street) and Abergavenny; the three variously served the N&W line between Pontrilas and Caerleon. The early 1960s saw the introduction of schemes for improved transit times by movement by road from the main railhead to the sub-depots (e.g. Newport to Pontypool Crane Street) from where the ultimate delivery (and initial collections) were made. However, this soon became direct delivery to final destination from the main railhead depot (e.g. Newport to customer) and goods and full load C&D services were all concentrated at Newport High Street. Domestic coal remained at almost all depots after the goods was removed, but under Coal Concentration developments, larger (partly) mechanised depots were set up, in the case of the Newport area at Newport Dock Street which opened in 1965, dealing with domestic coal traffic for all the surrounding area.

The introduction of the National Sundries Plan in 1965 saw all remaining depots open for Goods traffic split between Main and Secondary Depots. Cardiff Newtown and Swansea became the only two Main Depots in South Wales, with Newport as a Secondary. Newport continued to handle traffic for Pontypool, but those depots that were unable to load direct to Newport now had to load to Cardiff for transhipment on to Newport. In this arrangement, Newport had to send all outwards traffic (that they could not load away direct) to Cardiff for transhipment, a situation that caused considerable industrial unrest between the two depots.

Goods traffic generally became a very problematic low-quality and high-cost traffic for the British Railways Board, and a policy decision was taken in 1972 to cease carrying small goods traffic, from when it passed into the hands of road-based companies.

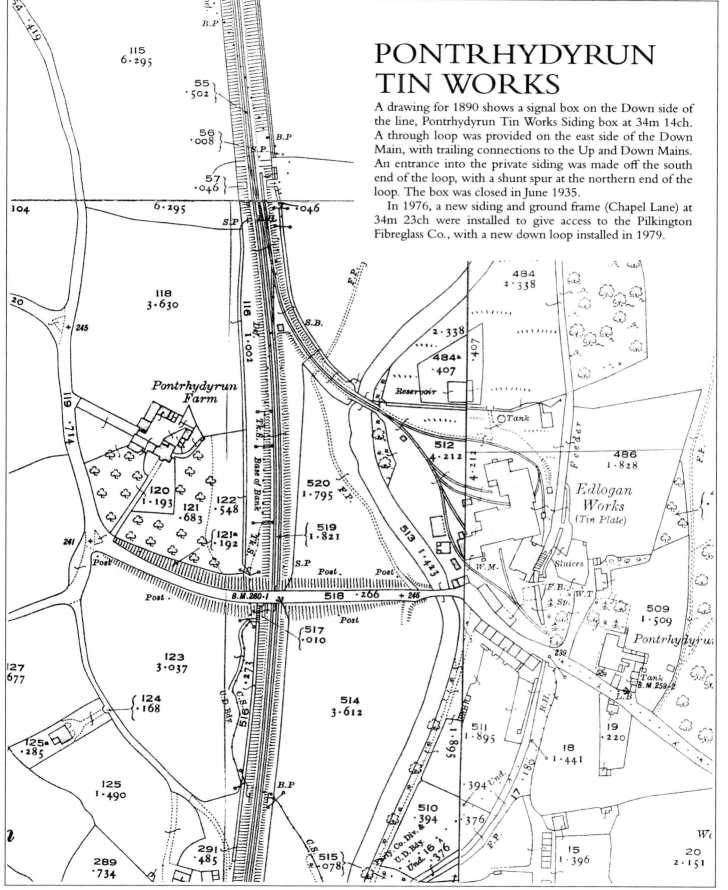

PONTRHYDYRUN TIN WORKS

A drawing for 1890 shows a signal box on the Down side of the line, Pontrhydyrun Tin Works Siding box at 34m 14ch. A through loop was provided on the east side of the Down Main, with trailing connections to the Up and Down Mains. An entrance into the private siding was made off the south end of the loop, with a shunt spur at the northern end of the loop. The box was closed in June 1935.

In 1976, a new siding and ground frame (Chapel Lane) at 34m 23ch were installed to give access to the Pilkington Fibreglass Co., with a new down loop installed in 1979.

Taken from 25-inch Ordnance Survey for 1920. Crown Copyright reserved.

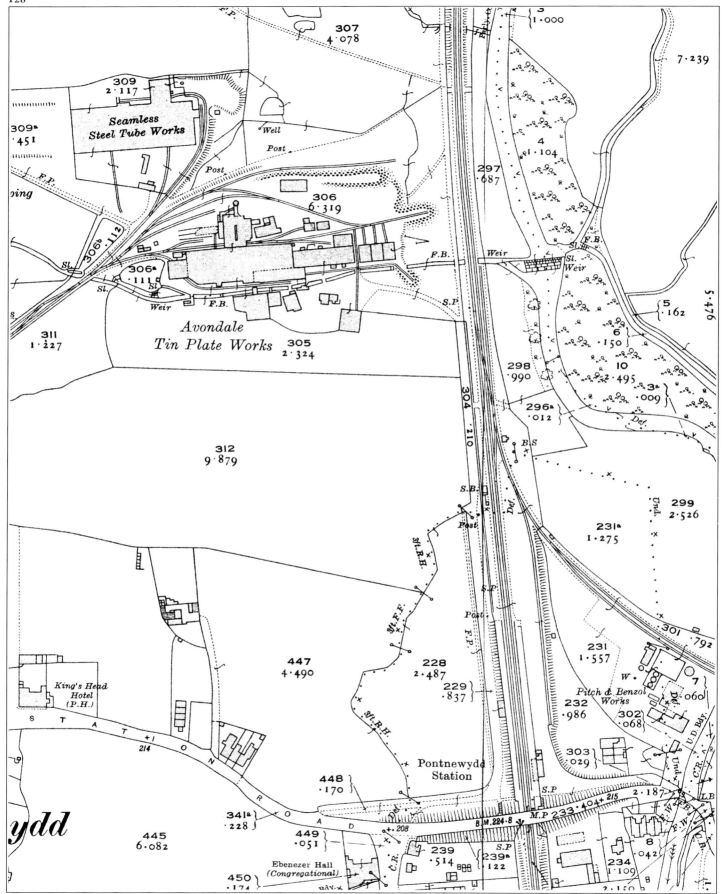

LOWER PONTNEWYDD

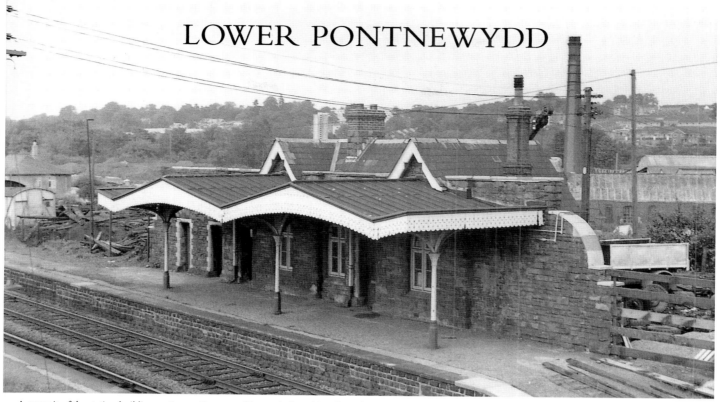

A portrait of the station buildings at Lower Pontnewydd, seen in June 1963 from the adjacent road bridge, some five years after closure to passengers. The buildings were on the Down side of the line, along with the goods facilities.
MIKE LEWIS

A drawing from about 1890 shows the station with Up and Down platforms at 34m 77ch. A goods shed was provided on the Down side, north of the platform, served by a loop with trailing connections to the Down Main on each side of the shed, and to the Up Main at the north end of the yard. One mileage siding was provided behind the shed.

Access into the private sidings of the Pontnewydd Tinplate works, which later became the Gwent Firebrick and Pipe Company, was also effected though the yard, but was closed by 1925.

Platforms in 1922 were shown at 335ft in length. A single 24-wagon capacity siding was shown on the Down side to the north of the station (off which the firebrick company's siding was taken), but no goods shed. A ten-wagon headshunt was provided at the north end, with trailing connections to each Main line below it.

The staff establishment at Lower Pontnewydd in 1929 comprised a stationmaster, a porter and two signalmen. From 1930, this was gradually reduced, and by 1934 just one porter signalman remained, supervised from Upper Pontnewydd (Eastern Valley).

Lower Pontnewydd station was closed in June 1958, whilst the goods siding remained in use until September 1965, when it was closed along with the signal box.

A view of the forecourt of the station when in use as a scrap-yard. The Up side platform building features in the background.
MIKE LEWIS

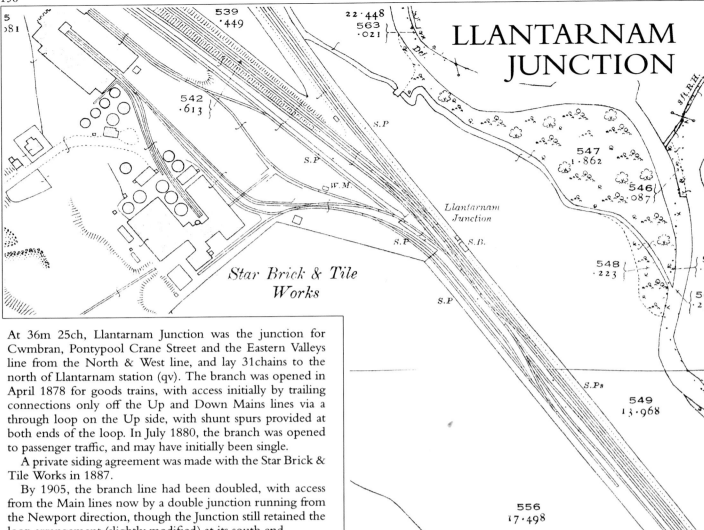

5
581

539
·449

542
·613

22·448
563
·021

LLANTARNAM JUNCTION

S.P

547
·862

546
·087

Llantarnam
Junction

S.P

W. M.

S.B.

S.P

548
·223

5
·0

56
·23

S.P

Star Brick & Tile
Works

S.Ps

549
13·968

556
17·498

Taken from 25-inch Ordnance Survey for 1920. Crown Copyright reserved.

At 36m 25ch, Llantarnam Junction was the junction for Cwmbran, Pontypool Crane Street and the Eastern Valleys line from the North & West line, and lay 31 chains to the north of Llantarnam station (qv). The branch was opened in April 1878 for goods trains, with access initially by trailing connections only off the Up and Down Mains lines via a through loop on the Up side, with shunt spurs provided at both ends of the loop. In July 1880, the branch was opened to passenger traffic, and may have initially been single.

A private siding agreement was made with the Star Brick & Tile Works in 1887.

By 1905, the branch line had been doubled, with access from the Main lines now by a double junction running from the Newport direction, though the Junction still retained the loop arrangement (slightly modified) at its south end.

A new signal box was provided in 1913, now opposite the junctions, on the Down side. Shortly afterwards, an Up Goods Loop was opened in 1914 to accommodate 60 wagons in addition to engine and van. This loop, originating just to the north of Llantarnam station yard, was built straight into the southern spur of the through loop, and used its crossover to regain the Up Main. The spur thus absorbed was replaced by another, alongside the goods loop. The northern spur off the through loop was also utilised for refuge purposes by the early 1920s (but also designated as a 'ballast siding'), holding a train of 38 wagons.

There were three signalmen established at the Junction in 1929.

Two further wartime private sidings were opened at the junction, one for Metalitho Ltd. in 1939, off the north end of the northern spur, the other a Government Cold Store, off the replacement south spur, in 1942. Further north on the main line, on the Up side, Lucas & Sons had a private siding which was later taken over by Girlings.

A Down Goods Loop was added in 1941 as part of the upgrading of running facilities right along the N&W line, and this ran from a point to the north of the Junction box right down to the north end of Llantarnam station's Down platform. The loop accommodated an engine, 86 wagons and brake van from the main line, but 60 wagons on trains from

the Cwmbran direction, which was provided with a crossover onto the loop to the south of the signal box.

The Eastern Valley passenger services over the branch ceased in 1962, and with the onset of road haulage and MAS, the private sidings were gradually closed between 1965–68. The branch was singled in 1968, the main installation remaining being Hafodyrynys Colliery, which was a basic supplier of coking coal to the BSC at Margam in block trains of 21-ton 'Minfits'.

Following the closure of the Vale of Neath as a through route in 1964, coal from Llanhilleth to Hafodyrynys for washing and inclusion in the Margam blend needed to be worked via Rogerstone and Llantarnam Junction, and due to the incline north of that point, was conveyed only in 17 wagon trains.

The Down Goods Loop was taken out of use in 1964, but the Up Goods Loop remained available until the Eastern Valley branch through to Blaenavon was closed in 1980.

A replacement for Cwmbran Station was opened on the main line about three-quarters-of-a-mile to the north of the Junction in the mid-1980s, and is now served by main-line trains.

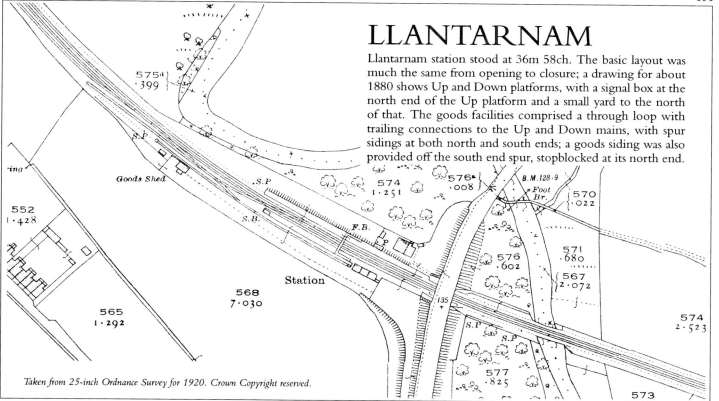

LLANTARNAM

Llantarnam station stood at 36m 58ch. The basic layout was much the same from opening to closure; a drawing for about 1880 shows Up and Down platforms, with a signal box at the north end of the Up platform and a small yard to the north of that. The goods facilities comprised a through loop with trailing connections to the Up and Down mains, with spur sidings at both north and south ends; a goods siding was also provided off the south end spur, stopblocked at its north end.

Taken from 25-inch Ordnance Survey for 1920. Crown Copyright reserved.

Llantarnam Station on Monday, 10th June 1957, seen from the A4042 overbridge looking north-west, with Canton 'Hall' No.6946 *Heatherden Hall* passing through with a Birmingham (Snow Hill) to Cardiff express. Access to the Goods Yard – beyond the footbridge on the left (Up) side – was latterly by a connection off the Up Main. Weston's Biscuit factory can be seen beyond it, with the advertising hoardings each side of the station building's chimneys. The station house features on the extreme right, off the Down platform.

MICHAEL HALE/GW TRUST

An Up Goods Loop was added in 1914 from a point just north of the yard as far as Llantarnam Junction, as discussed, accommodating engine, 60 wagons and brake van.

The station in 1922 was shown with 345ft platforms. In the yard, the northernmost headshunt/mileage siding had a capacity of nine wagons, and the southern of eleven. The spur off the latter, stopblocked at its north end, held five wagons, and was shown with an open 50ft goods platform and a goods shed/lockup on its south-western edge.

In 1929, the station staff comprised a stationmaster, three porters and two Station box signalmen From 1930, staffing was gradually reduced, and by 1933 only a porter signalman remained, supervised from Cwmbran; the signal box was reduced to a ground frame in 1933.

A new private siding opened in 1938 for Weston Biscuits, and was in use until 1966. To provide access, the north spur of the goods yard was extended into the Up Goods Loop, and the factory siding taken off this addition.

A Down Goods Loop was installed in 1941 between the Junction and a point just north of the Down platform, remaining in use until 1964, as discussed in the Llantarnam Junction section.

The station was closed to passengers in April 1962, whilst the yard sidings were taken out of use in 1963, but were then partially reinstated, and finally removed in 1977.

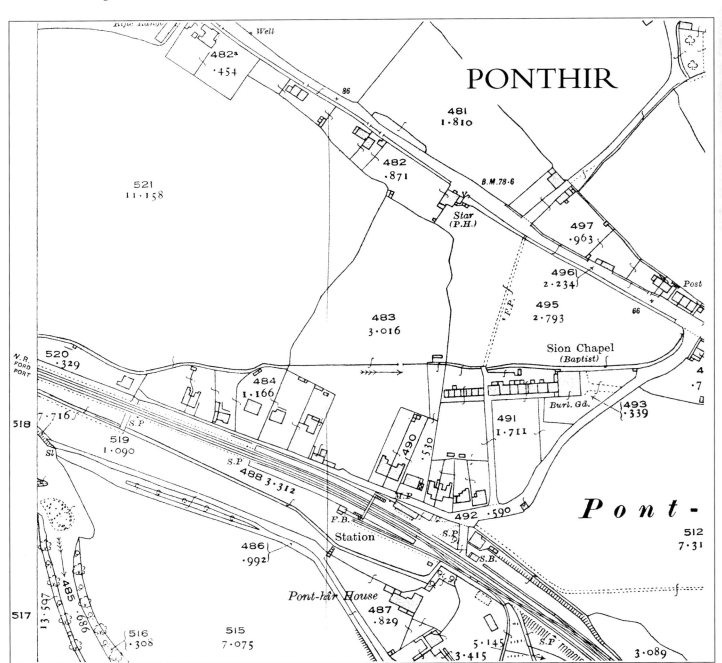

Taken from 25-inch Ordnance Survey for 1920. Crown Copyright reserved.

The short-lived 9.5 a.m. Birkenhead to Cardiff and 4.15 p.m. Cardiff to Birkenhead, a five-coach train worked by a Chester 'Modified Hall' from Chester to Cardiff and back, is seen here on its return journey just north of Ponthir station on Thursday, 20th June 1957. The train was worked almost every day by No.7922 *Salford Hall*, with 7921 *Edstone Hall* standing in as necessary, the former being pictured here. The weekday connection to Cardiff had formerly been made by a pair of coaches off the 9.20 a.m. Birkenhead to Bournemouth train, attached to the 9.25 a.m. Manchester to Swansea at Shrewsbury, balanced by coaches attached to the 8.55 a.m. Cardiff to Manchester.   JOHN HODGE

At 37m 78ch, Ponthir station had Up and Down platforms, with a signal box to the south of the station on the Down side. A drawing for about 1880 shows a small yard opposite the box, on the Up side, with a through loop and trailing connections into the Up and Down mains, and short spurs at each end. A private siding gave access to the Ponthir Tinplate works from the southern spur, but this had been closed by 1925.

A new signal box was opened in 1908, and lasted until 1961. Also in 1908, a new siding was added on the Down side, presumably to take traffic from the tinplate works.

The station in 1922 had 340ft platforms. On the Up side, the northernmost goods siding (partly behind the platform)

held nine wagons, and along with the tinplate siding still had connections to Up and Down Mains. Opposite, the Up siding (terminating near the signal box) also held nine vehicles.

Staff at the station in 1929 is shown as two porters and two signalmen, administered by the Llantarnam stationmaster, and from 1933 by Cwmbran.

Ponthir yard was officially closed for goods traffic on 9th June 1958, but by then there were no arrangements for delivering such traffic; all the goods sidings were subsequently removed.

The station was closed as part of the withdrawal of Eastern Valley passenger services on 30th April 1962.

Booked for a Canton 'Britannia' between Shrewsbury and Bristol, the 11.45 a.m. Manchester to Kingswear and Plymouth had nothing better for the journey than Cardiff 'Hall' No.6928 *Underley Hall*, on Thursday, 20th June. 1957. Seen here at speed just to the north of Ponthir station, the Plymouth express no doubt made its presence felt in no small way to the local residents, as the railway ran only a few feet from the houses along the roadway through the village.

JOHN HODGE

In the early 1950s, there would have been a good chance of seeing *King George V* on this working, but following its departure from Bristol Bath Road in October 1952, 'Castles' and 'Counties' were used on the turn, the 4.33 p.m. Bristol to Shrewsbury. This was the 10.5 a.m. Penzance to Manchester train, seen here on the southern approaches to Ponthir station. Currently with seven coaches, the train would be strengthened at Pontypool Road by the usual addition of four more from Cardiff to Liverpool which had passed Ponthir some fifteen minutes earlier behind No.5382. One of the two original modified double-chimney 'Counties', No.1009 *County of Carmarthen*, from Bath Road shed, is seen with that working on Thursday, 20th June 1957.

JOHN HODGE

Two light engines being returned from Newport to Pontypool Road shed are seen passing Ponthir box on Thursday, 20th June 1957. These are Pontypool's Stanier '8F' No.48424, and '2884' class 2–8–0 No.3813 from Oxley. Whilst light engine mileage was considered wasteful, it was necessary when a goods train had no suitable working back from a destination, and the loco had to be repositioned at another location in order to take up an appropriate service. This was not so apparent on passenger workings, where the engines' services were rather more balanced, and double-heading was used if necessary. Goods trains were more likely to be withdrawn, to run hours late, or be diverted to another destination, causing an engine imbalance, quite apart from the regular, scheduled light running that was often part of freight engines' turns.

JOHN HODGE

A slap on the wrist was due the Pontypool Road driver of this Ebbw Jct. '43XX' 2–6–0 No.5382 at the head of the 4.40 p.m. Cardiff to Pontypool fast, as he was still carrying the reporting number from the balancing Down service, the 9.15 a.m. Manchester to Swansea, which this engine worked from Pontypool Road to Cardiff earlier that day, Thursday, 20th 1957. This service, which conveyed the Cardiff to Liverpool through coaches that were to be attached to the 10.5 a.m. Penzance to Liverpool train at Pontypool Road, called only at Newport en route. The train was about to pass through Ponthir station, pictured alongside the small Ponthir signal box located off the south end of the Down platform.

JOHN HODGE

Ponthir Station was served mainly by the Eastern Valleys Newport to Pontypool (Crane Street) and Blaenavon services, which were worked mostly by '64XX', '57XX' or the larger '41XXs'. Here, No.6429 of Pontypool Road was hauling an auto service from Newport into the station on Thursday, 20th June 1957.   JOHN HODGE

Running through the station with the 1.0 p.m. Birmingham (Snow Hill) to Cardiff express on Thursday, 20th June 1957, the prototype 'Hall' No.4900 *Saint Martin*, then based at Old Oak Common, showed signs of high mileage since her last Heavy General in September 1955, and failed to live up to the normal Old Oak standard of cleanliness. The six-coach train was the usual formation from Birmingham for this service, though reduced to five during the winter timetable. In this period, it also conveyed four coaches from Shrewsbury to Cardiff, attached at Hereford, though these are absent on this occasion.   JOHN HODGE

Ebbw Junction's '51XX' No.5171 leaving the Down platform at Ponthir with one of the (approximately hourly) Blaenavon to Newport services on Thursday, 20th June 1957. These amounted to about 18 on weekdays and 8 on Sundays, although a couple of Hereford, Pontypool Road & Newport main-line stopping trains in each direction also called.   JOHN HODGE

The ubiquitous '57XX' panniers handled many services on the Eastern Valley, as seen here with Ebbw Jct.'s No.3714 on a Pontypool Crane Street to Newport train as it eased into Ponthir's Down platform on Thursday, 20th June 1957. Ponthir served a fairly sparse rural community, but its train service was quite excellent compared to such stations on the central and northern sections of the N & W, though only by the presence of the Eastern Valley services.   JOHN HODGE

12
·467

11
7·805

6
·985

5
·555

147
·474

Aqueduct

8
·492

7
2·127

144
2·357

Penrhos
Villas

9
919

140
61

50

146
·732

145
·648

143
·206

52

141
13·862

142
·279

Tank

Tank

F.D.

Kilns

Kilns

66

BM.67·99

Kilns

Kilns

Penrhos Works
(Brick & Tile)

BM.75·82

168
·956

167
·743

60

171
·487

F.B.

P

S.P.

Lower Malthouse

170
·982

Posts

S.P.

172
3·035

S.P.

169
·199

49

F.B.

166
11·464

F.B.

173
·571

S.B

Sl.

Greenmeadow

G.P.

50

F.Bs

209
4·135

58

Mill Race

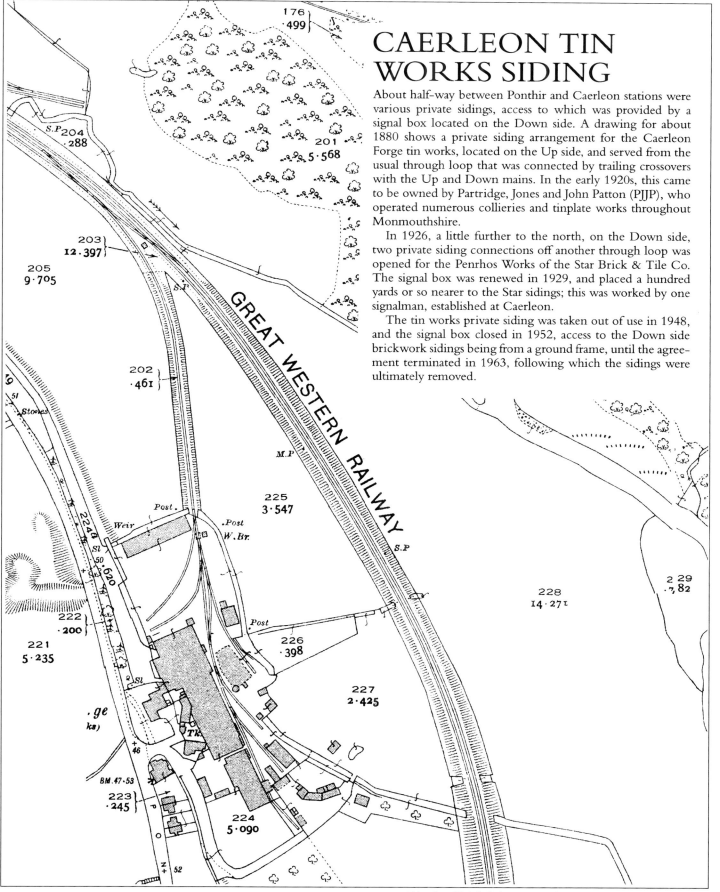

CAERLEON TIN WORKS SIDING

About half-way between Ponthir and Caerleon stations were various private sidings, access to which was provided by a signal box located on the Down side. A drawing for about 1880 shows a private siding arrangement for the Caerleon Forge tin works, located on the Up side, and served from the usual through loop that was connected by trailing crossovers with the Up and Down mains. In the early 1920s, this came to be owned by Partridge, Jones and John Patton (PJJP), who operated numerous collieries and tinplate works throughout Monmouthshire.

In 1926, a little further to the north, on the Down side, two private siding connections off another through loop was opened for the Penrhos Works of the Star Brick & Tile Co. The signal box was renewed in 1929, and placed a hundred yards or so nearer to the Star sidings; this was worked by one signalman, established at Caerleon.

The tin works private siding was taken out of use in 1948, and the signal box closed in 1952, access to the Down side brickwork sidings being from a ground frame, until the agreement terminated in 1963, following which the sidings were ultimately removed.

Taken from 25-inch Ordnance Survey for 1936. Crown Copyright reserved.

Photographed from the road bridge over the short section of the cutting to the north-east of the station, this modest class 'H' freight was heading south behind Severn Tunnel 2–8–0 No. 3866 on Thursday, 20th June 1957, probably bound for one of the Newport yards. The extent of the sharp curve may be judged by the fact that only about a quarter of it is seen in this view. No.3866 entered traffic in December 1942, the final member of her class, and spent her first three years at Canton before moving on to Oxford until February 1952, when she was transferred to Severn Tunnel Jct. Her very orderly train consisted of opens, oil tankers and containers.

JOHN HODGE

CAERLEON

Caerleon station lay on a tight curve, as can readily be seen in this study of the station looking Up towards Pontypool Road, taken in the early 1960s. The station was sandwiched between two bridges, at this time a brick-built structure to its north-east carrying the B4236, and a steel span to the south-west (behind the photographer) carrying a lane towards Malpas. The main station building was on the Down platform, on the right, as was the town, with a shelter on the Up, connected by a footbridge. The goods yard was at the south end of the Down platform, off to the right of this picture.
MONMOUTHSHIRE RAILWAY
SOCIETY

Working through from Cardiff to Shrewsbury with the 8.55 a.m. Cardiff to Manchester, Canton 'Britannia' No.70018 *Flying Dutchman* is seen passing through Caerleon station on Tuesday, 27th May 1958. She was due to return to Pontypool Road with the 11.45 a.m. Manchester to Plymouth, and home with the connecting 4.45 p.m. to Cardiff. At this point, the 8.55 was scheduled to consist of one coach for Chester and seven for Manchester (plus any strengthening), with five from Bristol to Crewe being attached at Pontypool Road. The rather unusual saw-tooth pattern of canopy at Caerleon can be seen here, a design more often associated with other railways, though it was used in various forms at WR platforms with a sharp curvature (Weston-super-Mare, for example).
R.O. TUCK

Caerleon station lay on a tight curve at 39m 41ch, with Up and Down platforms of approximately equal length. An 1880 diagram shows a small goods yard to the south of the Down platform, with a through loop served by trailing connections to the Up and Down Mains. A siding off the loop served a goods shed, and also a pair of sidings on the extended shed road.

In the post-Great War period, a mileage siding was added at the back of the goods yard.

In 1922, the station was shown with a 350ft Down platform, and a 345ft Up. The goods shed road held three wagons inside and three outside, with the shed siding alongside another four. There was a 30cwt crane inside the shed, and a 4-ton crane outside its north end, between the shed road and its adjacent siding. The two northern sidings off the shed road each held six wagons, with a wagon weighbridge on one. The new mileage siding to the east held 31 wagons. There was a trailing connection to the Up Main by the goods shed, whilst at the southern end there were two onto the Down main; the signal box and cattle pens sat alongside the headshunt road between two yard points for the latter connection.

The staff at Caerleon in 1929 were supervised by a stationmaster, and comprised:

Booking Clerk	1
Ticket Collectors	3
Porters	3
Goods Porter	1
Signalmen:	
Station	3
St. Julians	3
Charwoman	1

The Station signal box was closed in 1961 and replaced by two ground frames. The station itself closed for passengers in April 1962, upon the withdrawal of the Eastern Valleys services.

Goods facilities remained in use until November 1965, when collections and deliveries were made from Newport High Street.

Some 1½ miles to the south, just beyond the St. Julians River Bridge over the Usk, was St. Julians Siding box, which gave access to the St. Julians Brickwork Co. site on the Down side. This opened to rail traffic around 1894, and the box was rebuilt in 1907. St. Julians box was closed in January 1933.

REVISION OF 1936

MONMOUTH DIVISION

XXIX. 5.

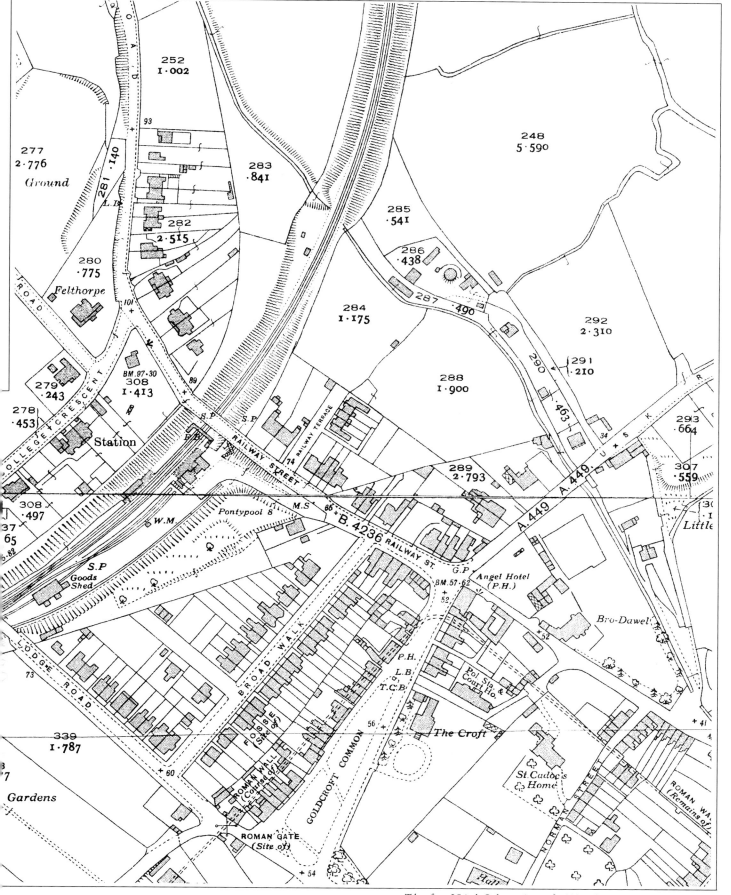

Caerleon's goods facilities remained in operation until 1962, with siding accommodation for a few years beyond that. Pontypool Road's '57XX' No.4668 is pictured in the short loop between the Down Main and the goods shed, seen on the right, on Friday, 19th May 1950. This was probably the 7.30 a.m. Pontypool Road to Newport (Ebbw Jct.) local freight, which was destined to call at Caerleon between 11.28 a.m. and noon to carry out work. F.K. DAVIS/GW TRUST

Oxley 'Hall' No.4997 *Eyton Hall* was an unusual engine to be working the 2.5 p.m. Cardiff to Hereford semi-fast on Thursday, 20th June 1957, and may have been a replacement for a failed Canton engine. She may well have worked into South Wales on a goods train, and been appropriated for a suitable movement part of the way back to her home shed. Her grimy condition supports the fact she would be at Swindon Works by the end of the year for a heavy repair. The trailing connection from the goods yard to the Up Main is evident in the foreground, completing the crossing just before the Up platform. A section of retaining wall was required at this point to hold the cutting. JOHN HODGE

The level of main-line express passenger services on Summer Saturdays along the North & West was considerably increased over weekdays, and here Pontypool Road 'Grange' No. 6871 *Bourton Grange* is seen at the head of the 10.4 a.m. Exeter to Manchester (London Road) service, which she would have worked either through from Exeter or Bristol to Shrewsbury on 26th June 1954. Though not advertised as such on the Western Region, the train started at 9.18 a.m. from Exmouth (SR), and formed a relief to the 9.5 a.m. Paignton to Manchester (London Road), which followed six minutes later from Exeter. Taken from the overbridge carrying the lane, there is a good view of Caerleon signal box, and of the straight that ran for almost a mile before it turned left to cross the River Usk and enter the northern outskirts of Newport. The southern part of the long cutting through the higher ground at Caerleon is seen (over a half-mile in total length), with the girderwork that carried pipes across the line in the distance.
R.O. TUCK

Seen from the steel road bridge at the south-west end of the station, looking towards Maindee on Thursday, 20th June 1957, the 7.30 a.m. Penzance to Manchester is shown sweeping into the curve through Caerleon. Chester 'Grange' No.6823 *Oakley Grange* and Canton's 'Modified Hall' No.6969 *Wraysbury Hall* were working between Bristol (depart 2.5 p.m.) and Pontypool Road, where they would hand over to a Longsight 'Jubilee' or 'Patriot'. The 'Grange' was being worked home from Bristol, and would probably take a freight northwards from Pontypool Road to Saltney. In front of Caerleon box, the trailing connection off the Down main line into the goods yard can be seen, with the double slip pointwork at its near end feeding two short shed sidings (right) and a mileage siding (left). The signal box closed in August 1961 under the Newport MAS scheme.
JOHN HODGE

MAINDEE JUNCTIONS

The three junctions at Maindee formed a triangle between the South Wales Main Line and the North & West route. Between the openings of the PC&N in September 1874 and the Severn Tunnel in September 1886, the junctions were used primarily for local passenger and goods, and some through freight traffic but, with the development of through fast passenger trains between the North, Bristol and the West from 1888 onwards, the East Curve became essential to the non-stop flow of the express services.

A drawing of the junctions in 1880 shows the tracks to have been double in each direction, with various engineers' sidings within the triangle itself, and signal boxes at the North, West and East junctions. Some ¼-mile north of the North box was Herberts Siding signal box, opened in 1878 and closed in 1907, which provided access to a private siding on the Up side which ran back onto a lower level where were located

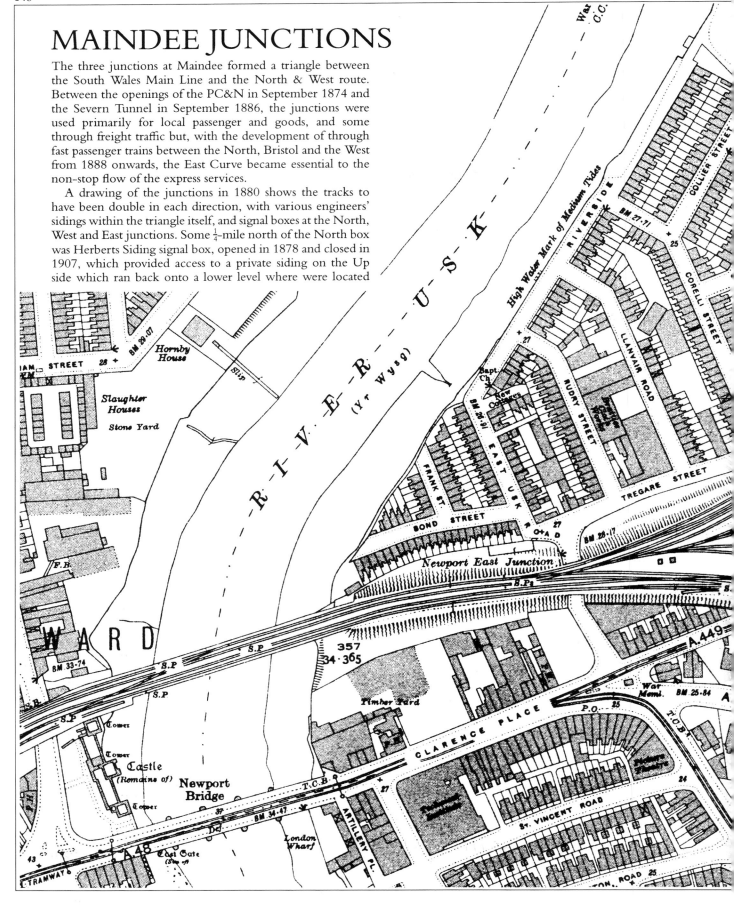